Ginger Up Your Cookery

Edited by Charles Seely

Decorations by Kate Simunek

Hutchinson Benham

London Melbourne Sydney Auckland Johannesburg

Hutchinson Benham Limited
17–21 Conway Street, London W1P 6JD

An imprint of Century Hutchinson

Hutchinson Publishing Group (Australia) Pty Ltd
16–22 Church Street, Hawthorn, Melbourne, Victoria 3122

Hutchinson Group (NZ) Ltd
32–34 View Road, PO Box 40–086, Glenfield, Auckland 10

Hutchinson Group (SA) Pty Ltd
PO Box 337, Bergvlei 2012, South Africa

First published 1977
© Text Charles Seely 1977, 1985
© Illustrations Hutchinson Benham Ltd 1977
Reprinted 1983
Revised edition 1985

Set in Monotype Times

Printed and bound in Great Britain by Anchor Brendon Ltd,
Tiptree, Essex

ISBN 0 09 159851 6

Contents

Weights, Volume and Temperatures

British Standard and Metric Equivalents

The quantities for recipes in this book are given in British standard weights and measures, likewise the temperatures and their metric equivalents.

However the reader may notice that in some instances metric equivalents are adjusted a little to make convenient quantities rather than being exact conversions from imperial units.

For exact conversions please refer to the conversion tables as below:

WEIGHTS

1 stone	=	14 lb	=	6.35	kg
2 lb 3 oz	=	1 kg	=	1000	g
1 lb	=	16 oz	=	453.59	g
1 oz	=	437 grains	=	28.35	g
1 cup	about	5 oz	about	140	g
1 tablespoon	about	$\frac{1}{2}$ oz	about	14	g
1 teaspoon	about	$\frac{1}{3}$ tablespoon	about	5	g

VOLUME

1 gallon	=	8 pints	=	4.55	litres
1$\frac{3}{4}$ pints	=	1 litre	=	1000	ml (cc)
1 pint	=	20 fluid ounces	=	568	ml
1 fluid ounce	=	8 drams	=	28.4	ml
1 cup	about	8 fluid ounces	about	227	ml
1 tablespoon	about	5 drams	about	18	ml
1 teaspoon	about	$\frac{1}{3}$ tablespoon	about	6	ml

TEMPERATURES

	Degrees Fahrenheit	Gas Mark	Degrees Celsius
Very slow oven	158 — 248	0 — $\frac{1}{2}$	70 — 120
Slow oven	248 — 302	$\frac{1}{2}$ — 2	120 — 150
Moderate slow oven	302 — 356	2 — 4	150 — 180
Moderate oven	356 — 374	4 — 5	180 — 190
Moderate hot oven	374 — 428	5 — 7	190 — 220
Hot oven	428 — 446	7 — 8	220 — 230
Very hot oven	446 — 500	8 — 10	230 — 260

All about ginger

Ginger was the first true oriental spice. For centuries it was brought from the Southern Asian fields across Persia on the Eastern caravan routes to Europe, where it was in great demand for its characteristic pungency and aroma.

The medicinal use of ginger was recommended in ancient Chinese treatises. Sanskrit literature described its pungent and aromatic spiciness when used in Indian cookery. Talmud and Koran scriptures described the use of ginger in a 'refresher cup'. In Arabia, ginger's aphrodisiac properties were advocated in the stories of *The Thousand and One Nights.*

The Greek philosopher Pythagoras recommended ginger as an antidote for sickness in combination with orris-root, gentian, black pepper and honey. It is also believed that the first recipe for gingerbread was invented by the ancient Greeks.

The Romans, with the help of Arabian traders, introduced ginger to the rest of Europe.

Later on, fancy ginger cake was a speciality highly esteemed by the Elizabethans. Henry VIII appears to have valued its medicinal virtues. Shakespeare mentioned gingerbread in *Love's Labours Lost,* which shows that it was known by the English commoner.

Ginger was used for centuries in taverns where customers would help themselves from a jar to add spice to their tankards of porter. The practice of keeping a pot of ginger on the bar only ceased just before the Second World War.

Ginger originated in the southern Provinces of China and in India, where it has been used in cooking and medicine for thousands of years.

The same Arabian traders who brought the spice to Europe took the ginger plant from India to East Africa where it is grown today. The Chinese spread their cultivation into the Malayan Peninsula. In the sixteenth century, the Portuguese explorers introduced the ginger plant to West Africa, and the Spanish *conquistadores* took it to the Caribbean. Both Jamaica and Nigeria produce ginger commercially today.

The most recent country to cultivate ginger is Australia. It was introduced by immigrants in the nineteenth century. The plant settled happily to grow on the southern coast of Queensland, where it found the warm climate and soil conditions the same, if not better, than in its native grounds.

The ginger plant

The ginger we eat is the root of a tropical plant botanically known as *Zingiber officinale roscoe*. In gardener's terms it is a fibrous-rooted herbaceous perennial, related to bamboo and indigenous to certain tropical regions where it grows abundantly in its cultivated and wild state.

The ginger plant has a white, pungently aromatic rhizome, covered with scaley leaves. The slender stalks are about 3 feet (1 metre) tall. They are encased by sheaths of light green leaves. Ginger is a little like a gladiolus to look at but with several spikes of flowers growing from one stalk. The flowers however, are not numerous. They are dusty yellow and speckled with a dark purplish-blue lip marked with paler spots. These flowers, especially in wild ginger, have a beautifully sweet perfume, a little like that of a lily.

The plant is propagated by dividing the rhizome. Different types of soil, climate and cultivation, in the countries where ginger is grown mean you can buy ginger of varying flavours.

How ginger is grown

Ginger is mainly cultivated in the tropics from sea level to 4,800 feet (1,500 metres). It thrives on rich, well-tilled sandy loams, with a good supply of humus. Ginger needs tropical heat during the growing season and some rainfall, though it cannot stand water-logging. It is a soil-exhaustive crop that requires heavy fertilization. Whenever possible, it is grown in rotation with other crops.

In Jamaica, ginger was traditionally cultivated on small-holdings on the soil of the virgin forests. Growers rarely used irrigation or fertilizers. Ploughing up the weeds and banana trash did not help in the long run and soon the soil became quite valueless. This wasteful method resulted in the production of large tracts of exhausted land. Probably this has been the main reason for the present decline of the ginger industry in that country.

The largest ginger-producing nation is India. Half the total world production is grown there. Most of the crop comes from the southern regions. Irrigation is still a novelty and is attempted only on a small scale in certain parts of the country.

Since practically the whole crop of Australian ginger is grown within a 30-mile (48-kilometre) radius of the Yandina ginger factory, an excellent extension service is available to growers, which not only assists in quality control of the cultivation and harvest, but also ensures that the latest agricultural developments are quickly implemented.

The drainage of the lower land, the extensive irrigation and fertilization of the ginger fields as well as modern agricultural techniques, correct the deficiencies of nature and virtually guarantee the Australian farmer a consistent ginger harvest in quality and yield.

How ginger is processed

For dry ginger, the rhizomes are lifted from the ground and then dried. The crudest way of drying is simply to put the roots out in the sun. Some ginger in India is peeled or uncoated of the outer skin before drying. Some, after peeling, is bleached in a lime solution. Those gingers are known as peeled dry ginger or bleached dry ginger. Cochin, the most superior Indian variety, is usually limed and is easily recognized by the slight lemon note in its aroma.

The ginger from Jamaica, which has a good reputation for its high quality, is carefully washed, scraped by hand and then dried in the sun. It is easily distinguished by its light cream colour, mellow taste and delicate aroma.

At one time African ginger was sun dried, completely unpeeled or only very roughly scraped. Today the quality shows considerable improvement, but it is still somehow brash in flavour, dark in colour and not so fine in aroma.

In China, ginger is bleached by washing in sulphur dioxide, or just by smoking with sulphur. This practice, although it gives an almost white product, makes it unacceptable on some markets.

Australian ginger is similar in flavour and aroma to Jamaican, but is coloured light golden and has a slight lemony flavour after grinding. It is processed by machinery. The closely controlled, fully mechanized drying and grinding operation gives a finished product of the highest quality and flavour.

Preserved and crystallized ginger, an ancient Chinese speciality, is considered to be a confection rather than a spice. Preserved ginger in syrup is prepared from fresh green rhizomes which have been cleaned, peeled, shaped and boiled in sugar. Crystallized ginger is similarly boiled. But it is cooked much longer until the sugar becomes dry. Originally ginger was preserved and exported all over the world only from Canton. Now the preserved ginger is prepared in Hong Kong, Australia, and in small quantities in Taiwan, Fiji and Mauritius.

During the last decade, the main development in the international ginger trade has been the firm establishment of the Australian ginger industry and its notable success in entering the world market. The success of Australian exports is the result of extensive research and capital investment, as well as careful control of production.

Research has helped the Australian growers to produce a virtually fibre-free ginger with a pleasant mild taste that makes it especially palatable. Modern equipment makes mechanized processing possible. This makes for high production standards and strict control of quality. New methods of storing, cooking and syruping have been introduced. These ensure that the ginger keeps to a consistent flavour when it leaves the factory, even though it is processed throughout the year.

The Australian ginger industry was begun commercially in 1941, when a few farmers founded an agricultural cooperative in Buderim, Queensland, to grow, process and market their ginger harvest. In 1950 they built a factory, the only mechanized factory in the Southern Hemisphere capable of processing ginger in all forms. In 1985 they transferred their entire operation to the new processing plant in Yandina, probably the largest and most sophisticated in the world, thus ensuring the continuing expansion of the industry.

It is now believed that Australian 'Golden Ginger' with its unique golden colour, its exotic flavour, distinctive taste, fibre-free quality and its freedom from impurities is unequalled the world over.

Preserved ginger has been previously categorized on the basis of a number of qualities, like 'stem' – the finest ginger made from the youngest growth of rhizomes, hand cut into plumlike shapes; 'cargo' –made from the remaining root after removing the stems; and 'shavings' – made from trimmings or any other ginger waste material. With the advent of the Australian product those categories have lost much of their significance. A greater proportion of the preserved ginger in syrup is now made to the specific requirements of the industrial users and to the demand of the consumers.

Fresh (or green) ginger is the untreated rhizome. About nine months after planting, fully matured ginger roots are harvested, then cleaned, bagged or crated and sent to the fresh vegetable markets.

The main suppliers of fresh ginger are Brazil and Central America with some from West Africa, Fiji and Hawaii. Australia also produces a considerable quantity – originally intended for local markets only but the increased plantations, coupled with greater world demand, has also encouraged Australian farmers to enter into the export of fresh ginger to Europe and North America, with considerable success.

Ginger in China

As the saying goes, the Chinese live to cook and cook to live, but their concept of a well-prepared meal goes beyond simple nutrition. They enjoy preparing various dishes which are praised for their nutritional, appetising and medicinal properties alike.

A light brown knobbly rhizome of refreshing but pungent flavour, which restores the appetite, aids digestion, prevents colds and alleviates nausea, has become, because of its culinary and medicinal value, not just a condiment or cooking ingredient but the basis of Chinese cuisine. Ginger brings a spicy characteristic of its own and yet readily mixes with other sour, sweet, bitter, salty or aromatic foods and in some instances mitigates their excessive flavour.

The Chinese use fresh ginger – sliced, shredded or minced – to cure or pickle any raw foods or to suppress a too-dominant flavour in meat, poultry or fish. They believe that ginger, with its pungent and very individual flavour, with its seemingly contradictory quality of being first warming and yet with a cooling after-effect, adds harmony and balance to various sauces and provides a refreshing counterpoint to fatty, savoury and rich dishes, adding a lighter note and an invigorating tang.

Chinese cooks mainly use fresh ginger which is gathered daily from back gardens or is obtained from local farmers at street markets. Only on the rare occasions when fresh ginger is not available will the cook turn to dry ginger. The ginger preserved in sugar, known as *marisan*, is usually served as a luxurious after-dinner confectionery.

A few Chinese recipes are included in this book. To get the best flavour the recipes should be made up quickly, served as soon as they are cooked and not kept warm in an oven for a long time. Chinese food is crisp and lightly cooked, so be careful not to overcook; its delicate flavour has made it the *cordon bleu* cuisine of the east.

Ginger in India

Both fresh and dry ginger are essential in Indian cookery but ginger as a sweetmeat is rarely used here, and then rather as a ceremonial confectionery.

The traditional meat dishes made from lamb and goat are cooked with lots of fresh ginger as it complements and counteracts their strong flavour.

Many of the appetising relishes, chutneys and pickles that accompany a wide variety of Indian meals are based on a mixture of fresh ginger and mango. Minced ginger or ginger paste is occasionally used on its own, sparingly in fish and vegetable dishes and very often with chopped onions and garlic as a base for the sauces; it helps to bring out the natural flavour of the foods and adds a tang to rather overcooked menus.

But the common denominator of Indian cooking is perhaps the imaginative, inventive and often unexpected use of spice mixtures, where dry ginger is a primary, pungent but refreshing and appetising ingredient. It is the blending of herbs, spices and seasonings as much as the meat, pulses, vegetables and relishes that gives Indian food its unique character.

In India the spices for cooking are prepared every day. The fresher the spices the sharper the flavour, so buy whole spices in small quantities and store them in jars or tins with airtight lids. This is much better than using ready-ground spices and it will help you to create a more authentic flavour when using the Indian recipes in this book.

Ginger in Japan

Ginger was probably introduced to Japanese food and medicine by the ancient Chinese, but in Japanese cuisine its use is mainly confined to the fresh product. They add freshly grated ginger with soya sauce to a variety of dips or mix it with rice vinegar to serve as a dressing with cold dishes. The traditional accompaniment to Japanese sushi are slices of pickled ginger (*gari*), as the Japanese believe that ginger cleans the palate and sharpens the appetite. Cooks in Japan use fresh ginger juice to season meats, especially their world-famous Kobe beef, and to counteract any unpleasant aftertaste. They also use shredded fresh ginger as a very important ingredient in simmered or steamed dishes based on fish or chicken.

Japan, together with China and India, probably accounts for more than half the consumption of the world's ginger.

Ginger from east to west

Originally, while the use of fresh ginger spread through eastern Asia, dry ginger became a feature of the cuisine west of India. In ancient times there was no choice as ginger could only be transported to the west in dried form, along the caravan routes, and the climatic conditions of the countries west of India were found unsuitable for cultivating this precious culinary and medicinal rhizome.

In the Middle Ages, English and Dutch sailors brought home from the Far East a sweetmeat ginger – preserved in honey or sugar – and in no time this exotic *marisan* became a fashionable after-meal dainty in both England and northern Europe; it was served as a sweet or as an aid to digestion after great medieval feasts.

Nowadays, immigrants from the Far East, having at their disposal modern technology in both the preservation and transportation of perishable food, import fresh ginger from their native countries to supplement their traditional diets and have introduced its versatility to local friends. This makes it plain why it still holds true that although ginger in all its forms is readily available in all corners of Europe, the dried variety is most widely known. The sweetened variety is mostly used in northern Europe and the fresh one is consumed mainly by Asian immigrants.

It could be said, however, that the English, Dutch and Germans are the biggest consumers of ginger in the west. They now readily accept fresh ginger in their diet as in the Middle Ages they accepted the sweet one and the dry one in ancient times.

Ginger in England

It is a common but mistaken belief that the British invented ginger wine, ginger beer and ginger ale, but ancient history tells us of the Chinese using ginger-flavoured wine in sacrificial rites, and both Talmud and Koran scriptures mention the refreshing and medicinal properties of gingered beverages. It is a fact, however, that ginger drinks were first adopted and then popularized in Europe by the British and taken by them to America.

It is also believed that it was in England that gingerbread was born. Alas, this has to be attributed to ancient Greece, but the British *can* claim to have brought a multiplicity of recipes for gingerbread and ginger biscuits into the world. One thing, however, is sure – it was in Britain that the first ginger marmalade was made and from here it continues to be exported round the world, as an English speciality. It could also be claimed that it was an English confectioner who first dipped preserved ginger in chocolate and it is still recognized round the world that chocolate ginger is a traditional English candy.

The British are partial to ginger as a flavour or ingredient in a wide range and variety of food, drinks and confectionery. In modern times, both the Indian and Chinese influences on cooking have brought in new ideas for the use of ginger in the English kitchen.

The coming of Australian preserved ginger, with its pleasant texture, has sparked off the recent increase in the consumption of crystallized and chocolate-coated ginger. Far Eastern immigrants, who brought fresh ginger with them to supplement their traditional diet, have introduced – and very successfully – this noble rhizome to the local cuisine, to the approval of the natives.

Today, ginger in Britain is fast becoming not merely an exotic Far Eastern speciality but an indispensable ingredient in the local cuisine.

Ginger in Holland

Today in the west it is not the Anglo-Saxons but the Dutch who are at the top of the ginger-addicts' league of Europe.

Holland, by retaining its close liaison with Indonesia for several hundred years, and having recently absorbed many immigrants, has consequently assimilated to a certain extent their habits and their love of cooking with ginger.

Besides dishes of obvious Indonesian influence, the Dutch have made unparalleled use of preserved ginger in their cooking and baking. There is no Dutch baker who does not jealously guard his own recipes for the world-famous *gemberkuchen*; there is no Dutch bar or restaurant which is not ready to offer their clientele preserved ginger with their drink, or with cheese, with ice cream or just as a cocktail nibble with pineapple; there is no Dutch kitchen or larder which does not hold one or two jars of their beloved *gemberblokjes* to supplement their daily diet.

The importing of crystallized and preserved ginger from Australia has heightened the popularity of this product as confectionery and the recent availability of good quality fresh ginger has added new applications of this rhizome in those dishes which call for appetizing, piquant but refreshing and sugar-free flavours.

The Dutch people's love of ginger leaves them with only one regret: that they cannot grow it at home and export it to the world, as they do with their tulips and tomatoes.

Ginger in Germany

Ginger arrived in Germany, as it did elsewhere in central Europe, via the eastern caravan routes, in dried form, and it became known there as one of the most versatile and widely used spices of all. German butchers have for centuries been using powdered ginger as a preserving and flavouring agent in their meat products, whether bratwurst, leberwurst or salami.

German bakers added the spice to a mixture of nutmeg, cinnamon and honey and so immortalized their own version of gingerbread, calling it *lebkuchen* and *speculatius*. Since the Middle Ages those little ginger cookies – plain, sugar-iced or chocolate-covered – in various shapes and forms, as gifts or souvenirs or commemorating civic or religious occasions, have adorned European festival tables, being praised for their exquisite flavour by children and adults alike.

The English and Dutch have tried hard to establish an export market in Germany for their ginger products but Dutch *gemberkuchen* and English ginger marmalade have met with mixed success – as foreign specialities rather than new German foods.

Preserved or sugared ginger was until recently little known in central Europe and whatever arrived from the Far East has gone mainly to the northern shores of Germany. But, happily, in the postwar years the situation has changed dramatically with the arrival of preserved and crystallized ginger from Queensland in this part of Europe.

The wide acceptance of the fruity, pungent but mild flavour of Australian ginger products, coupled with its medicinal properties, has ensured many German customers who, by tradition, are addicted to appetising and health-giving foods.

Although, as yet, ginger has not made a significant contribution to the German cuisine, ginger as a sweetmeat in many forms and as confectionery has become a fast-growing, health-giving commodity, available now in all parts of the country. As well, the recent appearance of fresh ginger on the market is giving rise to new experiments in the German kitchen, encouraged too by cookery writers in magazines.

Ginger in the New World

The multi-national exodus of Europeans across the ocean to seek new life and fortune in North America brought with it the habit of using dry ginger in cooking and baking. Later, African slaves and imported Indian and Chinese cooks used fresh ginger to create exciting dishes, marrying Old and New World foods to delight both them and their masters.

The Spanish Conquistadors, grasping the opportunity of newly created markets for ginger in this part of the world, transplanted this root from the East to the West Indies and then to Central and South America to establish a thriving ginger industry which still prospers today. Only Mexico shied away from ginger cultivation, preferring instead its old, hot favourite, the chilli. Thus Californians were forced to cross the Pacific in search of this noble root for the newly acquired taste for ginger flavour implanted by Chinese and Japanese immigrants.

American soldiers' contact with the Far East during and since the Second World War added a further stimulus to the popularity of this exotic spicy rhizome in the American cuisine, and today America not only uses ginger in all its forms but also grows some of the finest fresh ginger, in Hawaii, in an attempt to keep up with ever-increasing demand.

The evolution of Canadian society, similar to that in the USA, has been followed by a similar evolution in their cuisine, and now, as in the whole of America, ginger is no longer a foreign addition to the Canadian diet but a permanent ingredient in everyday cookery: California uses more fresh ginger than any other state, and Massachusetts more dry ginger, while Canadians from Victoria take their ginger in chocolate. Nowadays, in every corner of the New World, ginger has come to stay and is gradually being adopted into their multi-national cuisine to become an ingredient in the melting pot of the American heritage.

Ginger in Australia

Ginger also came to Australia with the immigrants. The saying goes that it was a Chinaman who was the first to plant this root in Queensland, in an effort to supplement his otherwise rather bland diet. The first ginger cultivation was either overlooked or ignored by the European settlers who preferred to import ready-made ginger products from their homelands. It was the Japanese blockade during the Second World War which created a shortage of this product and so turned the minds of the Australian farmers to growing this strange-looking but much sought-after Far Eastern rhizome.

The modern approach to the cultivation and processing of Australian ginger in Queensland has established, in a very short time, a unique ginger industry, anxious and willing to develop a ginger in texture, flavour and quality fit to meet the requirements of the western world – requirements which were to some extent ignored by the suppliers from the indigenous sources. The Queensland farmers have tamed the wild heat of Australian ginger and offer the world a mild, almost fibre-free strain of high quality which meets the most demanding standards of modern food processes and quality-seeking housewives in the west.

The development of exports has been going along in parallel with the development of the home market. Australia, which had been lacking its own traditional cuisine, was very susceptible to any newcomer willing to introduce new ideas, new dishes, new tastes and flavours based on native products.

The Chinese, being the most neighbourly and ingenious cooks, have had the most important influence.

No wonder, therefore, that since a home-grown ginger of high quality has been there for the taking, its popularity has spread through the restaurants and the home kitchen, from the most modern ginger processing plant in Queensland directly to the novelty-seeking consumer. Today Australians are surpassing Europeans and Americans in ginger consumption and the time is no doubt not far away when they will catch up with the ginger-addicted Far East.

Ginger in the kitchen

Around the world today, to 'ginger up your cookery' means more than just the addition of a racy spice with a volatile pungency to one's traditional diet. It is a rediscovery of a new exciting flavour, of appetising and stimulating dishes, and of a close encounter with the ancient high cuisine of the exotic East which now makes ginger popular the world over.

Choosing recipes for this book has been a difficult task for me and my associates as it was less a question of which recipes we could include, more a process of continuous regret over which recipe we ought to leave out due to lack of space.

Since 1977, when this book was first published, the popularity of ginger has grown dramatically. No longer is it a special luxury, or a romantic gift in expensive wrapping but almost an everyday foodstuff, widely available in all its forms. It is now found not only in delicatessens, but on many supermarket shelves and even among the vegetables on market stalls or just in the family corner shop.

1
Soups and starters

The recipes in this section have been collected from many parts of the world. Ginger is used to pep up the flavour of a carefully picked group of recipes, ranging from a quick melon starter to a spicy curried soup.

CHEESY CHEWS

10 dried apricots
3 oz (75 g) raisins
1 tbsp. mixed peel
3 oz (75 g) crystallized ginger

1 oz (25 g) walnut pieces
4 oz (100 g) finely grated cheddar
cheese

Chop the fruits, ginger and walnuts finely and mix in the cheese. Shape into balls the size of a walnut, using the heat of your hands to combine ingredients.

GINGER AND GRAPEFRUIT COCKTAIL

2 large smooth-skinned grapefruit
3–4 stems of ginger in syrup, sliced or shredded

Halve grapefruit and prepare in the usual way, removing all the pith. Hollow the centre slightly and then put 1 tablespoon of ginger with a teaspoon of the syrup in the centre of each half. Chill and serve in coupe glasses. *Serves 4.*

GINGER AND MELON CORONETS

1 medium-size ripe cantaloupe or
   ogen melon
sugar

a little sherry
4 oz (100 g) preserved ginger,
   finely chopped

Remove top from melon in a zig-zag fashion. Take out seeds, then cut centre pulp out. Cut into squares or balls. (To make balls, insert vegetable scoop into flesh. Turn scoop slowly and carefully to cut out a neat complete ball.) Mix with the ginger, adding a little sugar and sherry if wished. Pile back into melon case. Serve as cold as possible. *Serves 4.*

HOT MELON WITH GINGER

1 ripe melon
juice of 1 orange

1 tsp. ground ginger
preserved ginger (*optional*)

Slice ripe melon, remove the seeds. Moisten with orange juice, sprinkle with a little ground ginger and warm in hot oven for 5 minutes. *Serves 4–6.*

For non-slimmers: blend a little preserved ginger syrup with the orange juice and top with pieces of preserved ginger. Omit the ground ginger if wished.

LIVER PÂTÉ

1 lb (450 g) chicken livers
½ teacup dry white wine
½ teacup water
1 tsp. chicken-flavoured stock
   base or ½ chicken stock cube
1 tsp. parsley flakes
1 tbsp. instant onion flakes

¼ tsp. ground ginger
1 tbsp. soy sauce
2 oz (50 g) soft butter
1 tsp. Worcestershire sauce
¼ tsp. dry mustard
dash nutmeg
1 tbsp. brandy

Combine the first nine ingredients, bring to the boil. Reduce heat and simmer for 20 minutes. Cool livers in liquid, drain. Put livers through fine blade of food grinder or purée in blender. Add remaining ingredients. Beat hard until well mixed and smooth. If mixture seems too thick, add a small amount of the cooking liquid. Store in refrigerator in covered container for at least 24 hours to blend flavours. Serve on crisp, shredded lettuce with slices of thin toast. *Serves 4–6.*

PEACH GINGER COCKTAIL

4 peach halves
½ teacup seedless grapes
1 tsp. preserved ginger for each
   serving

2 bananas
½ teacup orange juice

Dice peaches and bananas, combine with grapes. Pour orange juice over fruit. Place in cocktail glasses, top each serving with finely chopped ginger. Just before serving sprinkle lightly with sugar. *Serves 4–6.*

GAZPACHO

2 onions, chopped
2 cloves garlic, minced
4 green peppers, chopped
5 tomatoes, chopped
2 tsp. salt
½ tsp. pepper

2 tsp. paprika
¼ tsp. ground ginger
2 fl. oz (50 ml) olive oil
3½ fl. oz (90 ml) vinegar
15 fl. oz (450 ml) water
1 cucumber, peeled

Combine onions, garlic, green peppers and tomatoes. Force through a sieve or purée in an electric blender. Add salt, pepper, paprika and ginger. Add olive oil gradually, beating steadily. Add vinegar and water and stir well. Correct seasoning. Place in fridge to chill for at least 2 hours, using a wooden or glass bowl; do *not* use a metal bowl. Add cucumber sliced very thin before serving. If desired, slices of toast rubbed with garlic may be served with the gazpacho. *Serves 4.*

ASPARAGUS SOUP

1 tin asparagus or small
    bundle fresh asparagus
8 oz (225 g) breast of chicken
knob of green ginger
2 pt (1 litre) water

1 tsp. brandy or dry sherry
1 tbsp. cornflour mixed with
    3 tbsp. cold water
salt

Slice chicken and ginger and boil in water with asparagus and with liquid from tin of asparagus. Simmer for 30 minutes. Add brandy or sherry, thicken with cornflour and cold water, salt to taste and serve.

When fresh asparagus is used, it should be cut into pieces one inch long and boiled with the ginger and chicken for 45 minutes. Do not put lid on saucepan as this causes green vegetables to lose their colour. *Serves 4–6.*

GINGER AND CAMEMBERT BALLS

2 oz (50 g) butter
3 tbsp. plain flour
6 fl. oz (175 ml) milk
¼ tsp. salt
pinch each cayenne pepper and
    white pepper
4 oz (100 g) Camembert cheese,
    chilled

1 egg yolk
10 pieces large diced ginger in
    syrup, cut in half
a little plain flour
1 egg, lightly beaten with 2 tbsp.
    milk
dry breadcrumbs for coating
oil for frying

Melt the butter in a pan and then blend in the flour and cook for a few minutes. Gradually add the milk and continue stirring over moderate heat until you have a nice thick sauce, then boil for a minute. Season the sauce with salt and the peppers. Add the Camembert cheese, cut into small cubes, and the egg yolk; blend well. Turn the mixture onto a floured board and refrigerate for one hour.

Using a tablespoon of cheese mixture at a time, shape it into small balls, one around each piece of ginger. Roll the balls in flour, dip in egg and milk and coat with breadcrumbs. Refrigerate for 30 minutes. Fry the balls in hot oil for about 30 seconds or until golden brown. Drain and serve hot. *Serves 4.*

GINGER SOUP WITH DUMPLINGS

2 oz (50 g) fresh ginger root
8 oz (225 g) brown sugar
30 fl. oz (900 ml) water

4 oz (100 g) self-raising flour
2 oz (50 g) suet
salt and pepper

Slice ginger root thin. Place in pan with water and sugar. Bring to boil, stirring, then cover and simmer for 14–20 minutes. Discard ginger. For the dumplings, gradually add enough cold water to flour and suet, kneading the mixture to make a dough that has the consistency and pliability of wet clay. Pinch off about 1 tablespoon of dough at a time and roll it between palms of hands to make a ball. Place on waxed paper. Bring soup to boil. Drop dough balls in and cook 5–10 minutes over medium heat. *Serves 6.*

KNEIDLECH WITH CHICKEN SOUP

5 oz (150 g) medium matzo meal
salt and pepper
1 tbsp. ground almonds
pinch of ground ginger
8 tbsp. boiling water

1 egg, beaten
1 tbsp. liquid chicken fat
  (melted from raw chicken fat)
35 fl. oz (1 litre) fresh chicken
  stock

Place matzo meal in a bowl with seasoning. Sift in ground almonds and ginger and add water, egg and chicken fat. Mix well to soft dough that may be easily handled. With damp hands roll dough into balls the size of a walnut and place on tray or plate. Put this in the refrigerator for 30–60 minutes. Drop kneidlech balls into a pan of boiling salted water and simmer for 6–8 minutes, until double in size and light. Drain well, pour boiling chicken stock over kneidlech and serve. *Serves 4–6.*

GRAPEFRUIT SHELLS

Remove the core and pulp from halved grapefruits, sprinkle the shells lightly with sugar and fill with grapefruit and orange sections. Sprinkle the fruit with finely chopped crystallized ginger and refrigerate before serving.

CURRIED CREAM CHEESE AND GINGER DIP

8 oz (225 g) soft cream cheese
1 tbsp. finely chopped preserved
  ginger
1 tsp. curry powder
2 tbsp. fruit chutney

1 tbsp. desiccated coconut
pinch of salt
pinch of cayenne pepper
milk

Beat the cream cheese until smooth. Blend in the remaining ingredients and mix well. Stir in enough milk to make a dipping consistency. Chill. Serve with crisp fresh vegetables. *Serves 6.*

2
Meat

With its spicy taste, ginger can be used in many different ways to add extra flavour to economical cuts of meat. The Chinese and Indian recipes in this section introduce some unusual ideas for main dishes.

LAMB CURRY WITH GINGER

1 lb (450 g) lean leg or shoulder of lamb, diced
1 onion, peeled and chopped
1 tbsp. oil
1 rounded tbsp. curry powder (p. 13)
1 dessp. vinegar
1 level dessp. tomato paste
2 pieces stem ginger, chopped
salt and pepper
1 level tbsp. desiccated coconut

Fry onion in heated oil until golden. Stir in curry powder, cook gently for 2 minutes. Add meat and brown lightly. Blend in vinegar, tomato paste, ginger and a little seasoning. Stir well, bring to boil, cover and simmer gently, stirring occasionally to prevent the ingredients sticking. If the mixture becomes too dry, add a little water. When the meat is tender (about 1 hour), add the coconut and stir briskly until blended. Serve immediately with saffron rice. *Serves 4.*

LAMB CRANBERRY

2 lb (900 g) lean lamb, cubed
2 tsp. mixed seasoning
¼ tsp. black pepper
1 oz (25 g) instant onion flakes
¼ tsp. garlic powder
6 oz (175 g) can tomato paste
10 fl. oz (300 ml) red wine
15 fl. oz (400 ml) water
7½ fl. oz (220 ml) whole cranberry sauce
¼ tsp. ground ginger
¼ tsp. oregano

Trim off small pieces of fat from lamb and fry for 2 or 3 minutes to grease skillet. Add lamb cubes and brown on all sides, pour off excess fat. Add seasoning, pepper, onions, garlic powder, tomato paste, wine and water. Cover and simmer 45 minutes. Add cranberry sauce, ginger and oregano and simmer 45 minutes longer or until meat is tender. Add additional water if sauce becomes too thick. Serve hot over rice. *Serves 4–6.*

PAKISTANI KURMA CURRY

d shoulder of lamb
riander
ardamom
eeds
cinnamon
d cloves
1 tsp. o.. pepper
½ tsp. salt

2 in. (5 cm) piece green ginger
4 cloves garlic
1 onion, finely chopped
5 fl. oz (150 ml) yoghurt
2 oz (50 g) butter
1 onion, sliced
2 oz (50 g) almonds, slivered

Cut lamb into 1 in. (2 cm) cubes. Combine all spices, seasoning, finely chopped ginger, crushed garlic, chopped onion and yoghurt. Leave meat in this marinade several hours. Heat butter, fry sliced onion until golden; remove, then fry almonds, remove and reserve with onion rings for garnish. Drain meat, reserving marinade, add meat to pan and brown well. Add marinade, stir well, cover and simmer 45 minutes to 1 hour, or until meat is tender. Garnish with the fried onion rings and almonds. Serve with rice. *Serves 4–6.*

SHAMI KEBABS

1 lb (450 g) lean mutton or beef,
  finely minced
1 green chilli, seeds removed
  and flesh chopped
1 tsp. garam masala (p. 13)
1 in. (2 cm) piece green ginger, grated
1 tsp. salt

1 medium-size onion, finely chopped
1 medium-size potato, peeled,
  boiled and mashed
1 dessp. thick infusion of tamarind
  (p. 13)
2 oz (50 g) fat, or melted butter

Mix all ingredients (except fat) together. Shape into generous walnut-sized balls and flatten slightly. Heat fat and fry balls gently until brown and cooked thoroughly. Alternatively these may be slipped carefully on to long greased skewers, basted with melted butter and grilled until brown and cooked through. Set them a little apart from one another on the skewers. Turn and baste once or twice as they cook. Serve on a bed of rice with lemon and parsley. *Serves 4.*

SALMIS DE MOUTON

1 lb (450 g) lamb
3 lean rashers bacon
8 small onions
1 oz (25 g) butter
1 tbsp. flour
12 fl. oz (350 ml) ginger wine

5 fl. oz (150 ml) water
1 lb (450 g) potatoes
stick of celery
salt and pepper
garlic
a bouquet garni

Cut lamb into large chunks. Chop bacon and place, together with lamb and onions, into melted butter and cook until golden. Sprinkle on flour and stir. Add wine and water. Add potatoes, peeled and cut up, salt and pepper, celery, bouquet garni and garlic. Bring to boil and simmer for 1 hour. Remove celery, bouquet garni and garlic and serve. *Serves 4.*

BEEF WITH NOODLES

1 lb (450 g) braising steak
cooking oil
1 medium-sized onion, chopped
1 clove garlic, crushed
1 15-oz (425-g) can tomatoes
2 tbsp. soya sauce

½ tsp. finely chopped fresh or
preserved ginger
5 fl. oz (150 ml) beef stock
1 medium-sized green pepper,
deseeded and cut into short strips
1 tbsp. cornflour

Cut the meat into large cubes and brown in oil in a heavy-bottomed casserole. Remove the meat and put in the onion and garlic; stir well for a minute or two then add the tomatoes and their liquid.

Cook the tomatoes for 3 minutes, then replace the meat, stir in the soya sauce, ginger and stock, cover and simmer for about 1¼ hours, or until the meat is tender when pierced with a fork.

Add the pepper and cook for another 5 minutes. Mix the cornflour with 2 tbsp. water, add to the casserole and simmer, stirring, for another 5 minutes. Serve with boiled noodles. *Serves 4.*

GINGERED GOULASH

1 lb (450 g) diced pork or veal
2 tbsp. cooking oil
12 oz (350 g) chopped celery
4 oz (100 g) chopped onion
about 5 fl. oz (150 ml) water
12 oz (350 g) salted peanuts,
coarsely chopped

4 oz (100 g) finely chopped
preserved ginger
4 oz (100 g) deseeded and chopped
green pepper
a little pepper
2 tbsp. soya sauce

Brown the meat in hot oil in a heavy-bottomed casserole. Add the celery, onion, water, peanuts, ginger, green pepper and seasoning, cover and simmer for about 1 hour or until tender when pierced with a fork. Serve with rice. *Serves 4.*

KASHMIR CURRY

2 lb (900 g) boned shoulder of lamb
12 tbsp. sour cream
2 tsp. garam masala (p. 13)
4 tsp. curry powder (p. 13)
4 oz (100 g) butter
2 tbsp. blanched almonds
4 oz (100 g) sultanas

4 oz (100 g) dried apricots, sliced
4 cloves garlic, sliced
2 in. (5 cm) piece green ginger
2 large onions, sliced
salt
lemon juice

Cut meat into 1 in. (2 cm) cubes. Place in bowl with sour cream, masala and curry powder. Stir well and leave to marinate several hours. Heat butter in saucepan, fry almonds until golden, remove, drain and reserve. Fry sultanas and apricots until plumped, remove and drain. Fry garlic, ginger and onions until golden. Add meat and marinade, cook 5 minutes on medium heat. Add sultanas and apricots, cover and simmer 45 to 60 minutes until meat is tender; add salt and lemon juice to taste. Garnish with the almonds. *Serves 6.*

SATÉ KAMBING

3 lb (1·35 kg) boneless mutton, cubed
2 tsp. ground coriander
½ tsp. chilli powder
1 tsp. cumin seeds, pounded
½ tsp. saffron
1 tsp. ground ginger

2 cloves garlic, minced
2 tsp. salt
10 fl. oz (300 ml) vinegar
4 tbsp. groundnut or salad oil
5 fl. oz (150 ml) water

Pound together coriander, chilli powder, cumin seed, saffron, ginger, garlic and salt. Pound meat lightly and roll in spice mixture. Place meat in a bowl and pour vinegar, oil and water over it. Marinate for 1 hour. Drain meat and discard vinegar. Stick meat on metal skewers and grill until done (about 15 minutes). Serve on the skewers. *Serves 6–8.*

GINGER CUTLETS

8 small lamb cutlets
1 shallot
1 tbsp. Worcestershire sauce
4 tbsp. lemon juice
½ tsp. ground ginger

1 tbsp. soy sauce
½ tsp. dry mustard
1 tsp. chopped green ginger
1 tbsp. chopped parsley

Trim any excess fat from cutlets. Chop shallot finely and combine with remaining ingredients to make marinade. Soften cutlets in marinade for 1 hour, then grill until tender. Brush with any remaining marinade while cooking. *Serves 4.*

GINGERED LAMB RISOTTO

1 lb (450 g) lean lamb, diced
  (fillet, top of leg, etc.)
1 tbsp. oil
1 oz (25 g) butter or margarine
1 large onion, sliced
1–2 cloves garlic, crushed
2 large carrots, finely chopped

8 oz (225 g) rice
about 30 fl. oz (900 ml) stock
salt and pepper
½–1 level tsp. dried rosemary
2–3 oz (50–75 g) crystallized
  ginger, chopped
8 oz (225 g) frozen peas

Heat oil and butter in large pan. Fry onion, garlic and carrots gently until soft and just beginning to colour. Add lamb and fry gently for 10–15 minutes, stirring frequently to prevent burning. Stir in rice then add stock, salt and pepper and rosemary. Bring to boil, cover and simmer very gently for about 30 minutes, stirring occasionally to prevent sticking, and adding a little more boiling stock as necessary, until rice is cooked and liquid almost absorbed. Add ginger and peas and adjust seasonings. Cook gently for 5–10 minutes before serving. *Serves 4.*

SESAME STEAKS

1 lb (450 g) sirloin steak
1 tsp. lemon juice
1 tbsp. salad oil
4 tbsp. soy sauce
1 tbsp. brown sugar
1 tsp. onion powder
¼ tsp. black pepper
¼ tsp. garlic salt
¼ tsp. grated green ginger
1 tbsp. sesame seeds

Cut steak into 2 or 3 serving-size pieces, place in flat baking dish. Combine remaining ingredients, pour over steak, being sure to coat all sides. Let stand 1 hour or longer, turning once or twice. Grill 3 inches from heat a few minutes on each side until cooked – 3–4 minutes for rare steak, 5–7 for medium, 8–10 for well done. Serve with rice. *Serves 2–3.*

HONOLULU STEAK

4 fillet steaks 1 in. (2 cm) thick
1 tsp. grated green ginger
1 clove garlic, crushed
5 tbsp. water
1 tbsp. soy sauce
1 tbsp. sugar
½ tsp. salt
2 tbsp. red wine

Combine all ingredients, except steak, in basin, stir well. Add steaks and marinate for about 2 hours, turning occasionally, drain well. Grill or fry steaks until tender. Spoon the strained, heated marinade over as a sauce. Serve with hot rice. *Serves 4.*

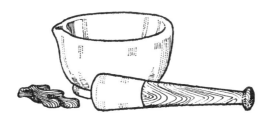

CHINESE GINGER STEAK

2 lb (900 g) rump or sirloin steak
1 oz (25 g) butter
2 medium onions
2 cloves garlic
2 in. (5 cm) piece green ginger
2 tbsp. soy sauce
seasoning
10 fl. oz (300 ml) water

Cut meat into strips ½ in. (1 cm) thick. Sauté sliced onions and crushed garlic in butter until lightly browned. Add ginger cut in matchstick strips, cook one minute. Add meat, soy sauce, seasoning and water. Bring to boil, reduce heat, cover and simmer 25 to 30 minutes or until meat is tender. Serve with hot rice. *Serves 6.*

HUSSAINY BEEF ON SKEWERS

2 lb (900 g) lean beef
3–4 small onions (cut in thick
  circles)
2 in. (5 cm) piece green ginger
  (cut in rounds)
2 oz (50 g) butter
1 tsp. ground coriander

½ tsp. chilli powder
½ tsp. ground turmeric
1 tsp. cumin powder
5 fl. oz (150 ml) water
¼ tsp. salt
5 fl. oz (150 ml) plain yoghurt

Cut beef in 1 in. (2 cm) squares and place on skewers, alternating with pieces of onion and ginger. Melt butter in a shallow pan and lightly fry spices. Blend in water and salt, add yoghurt. Put skewers in pan so they lie flat in this sauce. Cover with a tightly fitting lid and cook gently for 1 hour, or more, until the meat is quite tender. Eat with bread. *Serves 6–8.*

BEEF VINDALOO

2 lb (900 g) stewing beef
1 tbsp. ground coriander
2 tsp. ground ginger
1 tbsp. ground turmeric
1 tsp. ground cumin
salt

4 cloves of garlic, crushed
2 medium-size onions, chopped
9 tbsp. vinegar
3 tbsp. butter
6 bay leaves

Cut beef into 3–4 in. (8–10 cm) pieces. Make a paste of all the spices, salt, garlic and onions, ground down with vinegar. Rub this over meat. Leave meat in marinade for 24 hours. Heat butter and add meat with marinade and bay leaves. Simmer over very low heat until meat is tender and all liquid has gone. Serve with rice. *Serves 4.*

JHAL FARZI

1½ lb (675 g) leftover beef or
  lamb joint or cooked stewing steak
2 onions
1–2 cloves garlic
1 tsp. ground ginger
1 tsp. ground coriander
½ tsp. ground turmeric
¼–1 tsp. chilli powder
seasoning
1 oz (25 g) flour

3 oz (75 g) butter
20 fl. oz (600 ml) stock
grated rind and juice 1 lemon
1 tbsp. sweet chutney
½–1 tsp. garam masala (p. 13)
1 tbsp. apricot jam
2 oz (50 g) sultanas
1–2 tbsp. coconut milk
2 oz (50 g) blanched almonds

Cut meat into neat pieces. Blend chopped onions and crushed garlic with spices, seasoning and flour, then fry mixture in hot butter for 10 minutes, stirring well. Blend in stock, lemon rind and juice, chutney, garam masala, jam and sultanas. Add a little coconut milk, the cooked meat and season. Mixture should be fairly thick. Cover pan tightly and simmer gently for 1½ hours, stirring from time to time and adding a little extra stock if necessary; stir in nuts. *Serves 6.*

BEEF CURRY WITH ONIONS

1½ lb (725 g) stewing steak
1–2 tbsp. curry powder (p. 13)
½ clove garlic, crushed
2 tbsp. oil
seasoning
1 tin sliced green ginger

4 medium onions
1 tbsp. soy sauce
10 fl. oz (300 ml) beef stock
2–3 tbsp. cold water
1 tbsp. cornflour

Stir curry powder in centre of large frying pan over low heat. Add garlic and oil, seasoning and ginger, mix well and cook for one minute. Add steak, brown on all sides. Cut onions into thin strips, add to pan, stir and cook until tender. Add soy sauce and stock. Cover pan and simmer for an hour or until meat is tender. Blend cornflour and cold water, stir into meat mixture and bring to the boil, stirring all the time until sauce thickens. Serve with hot rice. *Serves 4–6.*

ORIENTAL BEEF

8 oz (225 g) beef
1½ oz (37 g) bamboo shoots
2 oz (50 g) water chestnuts
2 oz (50 g) mushrooms
½ oz (12 g) grated parsnip
½ oz (12 g) green ginger

salt and pepper
1 dessp. sugar
½ tsp. sesame oil
1 dessp. sherry
1 dessp. soy sauce
1 tsp. cornflour

Cut all ingredients into small pieces. Place beef on large dish. Add vegetables, then add salt, pepper, sugar, sesame oil, sherry, soy sauce and cornflour (diluted in enough water to make a thin paste). Mix well and put over the beef. Place the dish in a pan of hot water and steam for 10 minutes. *Serves 3–4.*

GINGER PINEAPPLE MEAT BALLS

1 lb (450 g) minced beef
15 oz (425 g) tin pineapple
6 gingernut biscuits
1 onion, grated
7½ oz (220 g) ready cooked rice
4 tbsp. wholemeal flour

1 egg
1 level tsp. salt
¼ tsp. pepper
2 beef stock cubes
1 tbsp. raisins

Drain syrup from pineapple and crush. Mix syrup with water and pour on to broken biscuits in a large saucepan and allow to soak. Mix beef with onion, rice, wholemeal flour, egg, salt and pepper. Shape into 1 in. (2 cm) balls. Add stock cubes, raisins and crushed pineapple to soaking biscuits and bring to boil, stirring constantly. Reduce to simmering and add meat balls. Cook uncovered over low heat for 10 minutes. Carefully turn balls and cook for a further 10 minutes. Serve on hot fluffy rice. *Serves 4.*

SWEET AND SOUR PORK

2 lb (900 g) lean pork
10 fl. oz (300 ml) water
6 whole cloves
2 oz (50 g) butter
8 oz (225 g) brown sugar
2 oz (50 g) arrowroot
2 tbsp. vinegar
15 fl. oz (400 ml) pineapple juice
½ tsp. onion powder

½ tsp. ground ginger
1 green pepper
1 carrot
medium onion, sliced
2 tbsp. butter or margarine
2 tbsp. soy sauce
2 tbsp. cornflour
5 fl. oz (150 ml) cooking oil

Cut pork into pieces about ¾ in. (2 cm) thick and 2 in. (5 cm) long. Place in pan with water and cloves and bring to boil. Reduce heat and cook 25 minutes or until tender. Pour off water. Cool meat. While meat is cooking, combine the next seven ingredients, cook over low heat until thickened, stirring constantly. Cut green pepper into large pieces and carrot into thin slices, sauté with onion in butter for 1 to 2 minutes, stirring once or twice. Remove from pan. Mix soy sauce and cornflour until smooth. Pour over the cooled pork, toss to coat pieces of pork. Heat oil in pan and fry pork until crisp and brown. Combine meat, vegetables and sauce. Serve piping hot with rice as side dish. *Serves 4–6.*

CHINESE PORK

1 lb (450 g) pork
1 small cauliflower
1 dessp. soy sauce
1 dessp. sherry
pinch salt
1 dessp. oil

2 tsp. finely grated green ginger
12 walnut halves
15 fl. oz (400 ml) water
2 tsp. arrowroot
little cold water

Break cauliflower into florets, parboil for five minutes, drain. Slice pork into thin strips. Mix together soy sauce, sherry, salt and meat. Heat oil, fry ginger and walnuts over medium heat for two minutes, remove walnuts. Add meat and marinade to pan, fry until meat is almost cooked (approx. 10 to 15 minutes). Add cauliflower and water, simmer five minutes. Blend arrowroot in little cold water, add to meat, bring to the boil, boil one minute stirring constantly. Add walnuts. Serve with boiled rice and parsley. *Serves 4.*

CÔTÉS DE PORC À LA FLAMANDE

4 pork chops
salt and pepper
2 oz (50 g) butter

3 cooking apples
cinnamon
1 glass ginger wine

Season chops with salt and pepper and brown in butter. Take them out. Peel, core and slice the apples, and toss them in butter without browning them. Add a pinch of cinnamon. Put chops on apple. Sprinkle on the ginger wine. Put tiny piece of butter on each chop. Place in casserole with lid. Cook for 30 minutes at 350°F (180°C), Gas Mark 4. *Serves 4.*

SUGARED PORK

1 pork joint about 3½ lb (1·75 kg) or larger
salt and pepper
2 tbsp. fat
20 fl. oz (600 ml) ginger wine
2 tbsp. syrup
2 tbsp. granulated sugar
thin slices of orange and sprigs of parsley to garnish
2 shallots (optional)
5 chestnuts

Rub meat well with salt and pepper and brown in hot fat. Add ginger wine, syrup and just enough boiling water to half cover. Cover pan and simmer until tender, turning every five minutes at first and then every ten minutes so that ginger wine and syrup can penetrate meat. Cooking time is 30 minutes per pound (65 per kg). When tender, remove from pan, sprinkle with sugar and set under grill until a crust forms. Garnish with slices of orange and parsley sprigs.

For sauce: chop shallots finely and put into saucepan with sauce in which the pork has been cooked, bring to boil and reduce until syrupy. Add sliced chestnuts and cook for about 20 minutes. *Serves 6 or more, depending on size of joint.*

HONEY-GLAZED PORK SHOULDER

4 lb (1·8 kg) pork shoulder
2 tsp. salt
1 tbsp. mixed seasoning
½ tsp. garlic powder
¼ tsp. black pepper
2 tbsp. honey
½ tsp. ground ginger
½ tsp. powdered horseradish

Thoroughly rub pork with mixture of salt, seasoning, garlic, pepper. Place, fat side up, on rack in shallow pan. Roast 40 minutes per pound (90 per kg) or until meat thermometer registers 185°F (85°C) in oven 325°F (170°C), Gas Mark 3. Carefully remove skin and score fat in diamond pattern. Pour mixture of honey, ginger and powdered horseradish over scored fat and return meat to oven. Roast 20 minutes longer or until well glazed. *Serves 4–6.*

INDONESIAN SPARERIBS

3 lb (1·35 kg) spareribs
¾ tsp. salt
¼ tsp. black pepper
1 tbsp. coriander seed, crushed
1 tbsp. cumin seed, crushed
1 tbsp. minced onion
½ tsp. ginger
4 tbsp. salad oil
1 tbsp. brown sugar
4 tbsp. soy sauce
4 tbsp. lemon juice

Cut spareribs into serving-size pieces. Place on rack in shallow pan. Combine remaining ingredients, mixing well. Spoon or brush sauce over ribs to coat all sides. Bake in oven at 325°F (170°C), Gas Mark 3, for 1½ hours or until meat is tender and browned, basting with sauce several times. *Serves 4–6.*

CHINESE-STYLE SPARE RIBS

2 lb (1 kg) pork spare ribs
4 tbsp. soya sauce

5 tbsp. finely chopped preserved
  ginger
1 garlic clove, crushed

Trim off surplus fat and divide the ribs into sections of two ribs each. Mix all other ingredients in a large bowl and place the spare ribs in it to marinade overnight.

Next day, remove the ribs from the marinade and wrap in foil. Bake in a roasting tin at 180°C (350°F), Gas Mark 4, for 1 hour. Then unwrap, pour any cooking juices into the marinade and arrange the spare ribs on a rack over the roasting tin. Baste with one-third of the marinade mixture, return to the oven and bake at 190°C (375°F), Gas Mark 5, for a further 30 minutes, basting with the marinade every 10 minutes. Serve with the reserved marinade. *Serves 4.*

THICKLY BAKED HAM ORIENTAL

3 lb (1.5 kg) cooked ham, cut in
  slices about ½ in (1 cm) thick
whole cloves
2½ oz (60 g) brown sugar
1½ oz (37 g) finely chopped
  preserved ginger

4 oz (100 g) stewed prunes
3 fl. oz (75 ml) pineapple juice
3 fl. oz (75 ml) prune juice
3 fl. oz (75 ml) ginger syrup

Place the slices of ham in an ovenproof baking dish; stud with whole cloves, sprinkle lightly with brown sugar and finely chopped ginger. On top, place pitted prunes, flattened out, and pineapple slices. Pour the combined fruit juices and ginger syrup over the ham and set the baking dish in a pan of hot water, in an oven preheated to 350°F (180°C), Gas Mark 4, until the ham is baked through, basting frequently – about 45 minutes. *Serves 6.*

PORK CHOPS IN GINGER ALE

4 large pork chops
2 large onions, sliced
2 oz (50 g) butter
little brown sugar

1 tbsp. tomato paste
1 tbsp. flour
10 fl. oz (300 ml) ginger ale
salt and pepper

Sauté onions with half butter until golden-brown; remove and place in a casserole. Brown chops well on both sides in remaining butter, then place them on top of onions in the casserole. Scatter brown sugar on top. Mix tomato paste and flour together and add the ginger ale; pour this over the chops and season. Bake at 350°F (180°C), Gas Mark 4, for about 1 hour or until chops are tender. *Serves 4.*

ESCALOPE OF VEAL WITH GINGER WINE

4 escalopes of veal
1 oz (25 g) butter
8 oz (225 g) mushrooms, sliced
2 glasses ginger wine
5 fl. oz (150 ml) double cream

Cut escalopes very thin and beat well. Heat butter in large frying pan and cook the escalopes – about 4 minutes each side. Remove and keep warm. Add mushrooms and cook until tender. Add ginger wine and cook fast to reduce. Turn heat down and add cream. Let sauce bubble gently, then pour over the escalopes. *Serves 4.*

JAMAICAN CURRIED VEAL

2½ lb (1·25 kg) pie veal, diced
4 oz (100 g) butter
2 onions, finely chopped
2 tbsp. curry powder
15 fl. oz (400 ml) stock
1 tsp. salt
¼ tsp. black pepper
½ tsp. ground ginger
dash Tabasco sauce
1 tbsp. tomato sauce
⅛ tsp. chilli powder
4 tbsp. black treacle (molasses)
2 apples, finely chopped
8 oz (225 g) celery, finely chopped
2 egg yolks, well beaten
5 fl. oz (150 ml) cold water

Heat butter, brown onions lightly and remove. Brown meat and remove. Fry curry powder till dark brown, then return onions and meat to pan. Add stock, salt, pepper, ginger, Tabasco, tomato sauce, chilli, treacle, apples and celery. Simmer until meat is tender, about 30 minutes. Add more liquid if needed to keep meat from sticking but mixture should be thick when done. At the last minute mix egg yolks with cold water, add to curry, and cook for another minute or so to thicken. *Serves 6–8.*

CURRIED LAMB'S LIVER

2 lb (900 g) lamb's liver, diced
2 cloves
2 dried red chillis
1 in. (2 cm) piece ginger root
½ tsp. cardamom pods
2 tsp. coriander seeds
2 tsp. ground turmeric
½ tsp. ground cinnamon
3 cloves garlic
4 tbsp. vegetable oil
2 onions, finely chopped
5 fl. oz (150 ml) yoghurt
10 fl. oz (300 ml) water
1 tsp. salt

Grind all spices and garlic together in a mortar. Heat oil and brown onions. Remove onions from pan. In remaining oil, brown the spices. Return browned onions to pan and add yoghurt, water and salt. Add meat last and simmer until tender, about 30 minutes. *Serves 8.*

LIVER WITH GINGER WINE

1 lb (450 g) calf's liver
flour
salt and pepper

3 oz (75 g) butter
1 glass ginger wine
5 tbsp. cream

Cut liver in thin slices about as big as sardines. Roll pieces in flour, season and brown them in butter. Add ginger wine and let sauce bubble for a few minutes, then add cream and simmer for one or two minutes. Do not over-cook. *Serves 4.*

RUMAKI

1 lb (450 g) chicken livers
1 tsp. mixed seasoning
¼ tsp. black pepper
⅛ tsp. ground ginger

2 5 oz (150 g) tins water chestnuts
1 lb (450 g) bacon
fat for deep frying

Cut livers into sections. Mix seasoning, pepper and ginger and sprinkle over livers. Pierce livers 2 or 3 times with fork to prevent excess popping. Slice large chestnuts in half and cut slices of bacon in half. Wrap one section of liver and one slice of water chestnut with a strip of bacon and fasten with a toothpick. Fry in deep fat, 350°F (180°C) until golden brown, or broil if preferred. Serve piping hot with hot mustard. *Makes about 30.*

FRIED KIDNEY

12 oz (350 g) kidney
1 dessp. cornflour
1 dessp. brandy
pinch powdered ginger

1 oz (25 g) oil
1 tbsp. soy sauce
8 oz (225 g) celery
4 spring onions

Trim kidney and cut into thin slices. Mix with cornflour, brandy and ginger. Fry in oil over high flame for 5 minutes, stirring constantly. Add soy sauce, stir and serve at once, garnished with celery and onions. *Serves 4.*

MEAT AND GINGER PIE

4 oz (100 g) spaghetti
8 oz (225 g) cooked minced meat
1 lightly beaten egg
2 tbsp. finely chopped preserved
   ginger
2 tbsp. grated onion

1 chopped red pepper
10 fl. oz (300 ml) milk
1 tsp. soya sauce
1 oz (25 g) breadcrumbs mixed
   with 1½ tsp. melted butter

Cook the spaghetti in boiling salted water until tender, drain and mix with the minced meat. Add all other ingredients, with the exception of the bread-crumbs, to the milk and pour this over the meat and spaghetti mixture.

Turn into a deep, well-greased ovenproof baking dish. Cover with the buttered breadcrumbs and bake in a moderate oven, 180°C (350°F), Gas Mark 4, for 20 minutes. *Serves 4.*

3
Poultry and eggs

Add ginger in its several forms to vary the flavour of economical buys like chicken and eggs. It helps you to turn a simple dish into something a little more exotic.

ASSAMEE CHICKEN CURRY

3 lb (1·35 kg) chicken
2 oz (50 g) butter
salt to taste
1 tsp. ground black pepper
2–3 bay leaves
1 tsp. ground turmeric
pinch chilli powder
¾ tsp. ground cardamom
½ tsp. ground cumin

½ tsp. ground coriander
¾ tsp. ground ginger
2 1 in. (2 cm) pieces cinnamon
6–8 cloves of garlic, crushed
1 in. (2 cm) piece green ginger
½ tsp. ground cloves
2 onions, chopped
30 fl. oz (800 ml) chicken stock

Joint chicken. Heat butter in saucepan, add all ingredients except chicken, chopped onion and stock; fry 5 minutes. Add chicken joints, brown well on all sides, then add chopped onion and cook gently, stirring occasionally, for 25–30 minutes. Gradually add stock, simmer 1 hour or until chicken is tender. Allow to cool. Keep in cool larder or fridge overnight. Remove any excess fat, reheat gently and serve with rice. *Serves 4–6.*

BRAISED CHICKEN WITH PEPPERS

3 red peppers
3 tbsp. cooking oil
1 tsp. salt
1 lb (450 g) boneless chicken
4 oz (100 g) finely chopped
  preserved ginger

pinch of brown sugar
2 tsp. sherry
1 tsp. cornflour
2 tsp. soya sauce

Core the peppers and cut into thin rings. Fry in 1 tbsp. of the oil, and the salt, for 1 minute. Add 2 tbsp. water, bring to a boil, cover and simmer for 2 minutes. Drain and set aside.

Cut the chicken into 1-in. (2.5-cm) pieces. Fry the chicken and ginger in the rest of the oil for 1 minute. Add the sugar and sherry.

Mix the cornflour to a smooth paste with the soya sauce and add to the pan. Heat gently, stirring, until slightly thickened. Add the peppers and cook for 1 minute. Serve right away. *Serves 4.*

SPANISH CHICKEN

2 lb (900 g) chicken
4 tbsp. olive oil
4 cloves garlic, minced
6 green peppers, diced
4 red peppers, diced
2 slices ginger
4 oz (100 g) bacon, diced

8 oz (225 g) tomatoes
1 tin tomato paste
2 tsp. sugar
2 onions, chopped
10 fl. oz (300 ml) chicken stock
2 leeks
1 lb (450 g) rice

Seasoning:
1 tbsp. white wine
¼ tsp. celery salt
pepper to taste

2 tbsp. sherry
1 tbsp. strong stock

Combine seasoning, rub well into chicken. Marinate for one hour. Heat oil and add garlic, green peppers, red peppers, ginger, bacon, tomatoes and tomato paste, mix well and add sugar. Then add chicken, onion, ½ stock and sliced leeks. Boil 10 minutes, place in well-greased baking dish with stock, cover and bake 1 hour at 350°F (180°C), Gas Mark 4, until chicken is tender. Serve on bed of fresh boiled rice. *Serves 4.*

GRAPEFRUIT AND GINGER CHICKEN

4 large chicken joints
2 oz (50 g) seasoned flour
2 tsp. ground ginger
2 oz (50 g) butter

2 tsp. oil
12 fl. oz (375 ml) grapefruit juice
5 fl. oz (150 ml) single cream

Toss the chicken in the seasoned flour mixed with the ground ginger. Melt the butter with the oil in a heavy pan. Quickly fry the chicken joints until golden brown on both sides.

Remove the chicken and blend in the remaining flour with the butter in the pan. Gradually add the grapefruit juice and bring to the boil, stirring all the time. Replace the chicken joints, cover and simmer for 40 minutes.

Place the chicken on a serving dish. Stir the cream into the sauce, heat through gently and pour over the chicken. *Serves 4.*

CHICKEN SALAD CANTONESE

8 oz (225 g) cold, cooked macaroni
1½ lb (675 g) diced cooked chicken
5 sticks celery, chopped
3 tbsp. minced onion

1 tbsp. finely chopped preserved
  ginger
salt and pepper
about 5 fl. oz (150 ml) mayonnaise
crisp lettuce leaves for serving

Combine the macaroni with the diced chicken, celery and onion and the preserved ginger and season to taste. Mix gently, together with the mayonnaise, and serve with crisp lettuce leaves. *Serves 6.*

ATLANTIC CHICKEN

4 chicken portions
2 tbsp. dripping or oil
2 large sticks celery, sliced
1 large onion, peeled and sliced
1 small green pepper, deseeded
   and cut into strips

1½–2 oz (37–50 g) preserved
   ginger, chopped
1 tbsp. ginger syrup
10 fl. oz (300 ml) chicken stock
salt and pepper
1½ level tsp. cornflour

Season chicken and fry in dripping until brown. Remove to shallow casserole. Fry celery and onion until soft. Drain off remaining fat, add pepper to pan and fry for 2–3 minutes. Add ginger, syrup, stock and seasonings and bring to boil. Pour over chicken, cover and cook at 350°F (180°C), Gas Mark 4, for 50–60 minutes until tender. Blend cornflour in a little cold water and add to casserole. Boil for 2 minutes. Adjust seasonings and serve. *Serves 4.*

TANDOORI CHICKEN

2 lb (900 g) roasting chicken
1 large onion
2–3 cloves garlic
1 in. (2 cm) piece ginger
1 tsp. coriander powder
1 tsp. cumin powder
¼ tsp. chilli powder

1½ tsp. salt
1 carton plain yoghurt
2 tsp. vinegar
2 tsp. Worcestershire sauce
juice of 2 small lemons
1½ oz (37 g) butter
1 tsp. garam masala (p. 13)

Make several cuts on side and legs of bird. Mince onion, garlic and ginger to paste, add coriander, cumin, chilli and salt. Beat yoghurt into vinegar and Worcester sauce, add juice of 1 lemon; mix thoroughly with spices. Rub into cuts and leave for 6 hours. Set oven at 325°F (170°C), Gas Mark 3. Melt 1 oz (25 g) butter in casserole and bake chicken with lid on for 40 minutes, or until tender. To serve, joint the bird, brush with remaining butter (melted), sprinkle with garam masala and the remaining lemon juice. *Serves 4.*

CHICKEN PILAU

1 medium-size chicken
1 lb (450 g) lean beef for stock-making
3 or 4 large onions, sliced
ginger
salt
8 oz (225 g) butter
2 or 3 cloves garlic
3 tbsp. stoned raisins

a few cardamoms
a few cloves
2 tbsp. blanched almonds
2 or 3 small pieces cinnamon
a blade of mace
peppercorns
8 oz (225 g) rice
saffron

Boil chicken in water with piece of beef, 1 or 2 sliced onions, a little ginger and salt. Heat butter in pan and fry rest of onions until golden. Add chicken and cook till well and evenly browned, adding other ingredients and spices, except the saffron. Add rice, saffron and chicken stock to cover. Put lid on pan and simmer very slowly. To serve, put the chicken on a hot dish and cover with the rice. Garnish with sliced hard-boiled eggs. *Serves 4.*

INDONESIAN CHICKEN

2 young chickens (about 2½ lb
    (1·25 kg) each)
3 tbsp. oil
2 tbsp. curry powder (p. 13)
4 onions
1 tbsp. green ginger
2 cloves garlic, crushed
2 green peppers, chopped
1 red pepper, chopped
½ tsp. ground ginger

½ tsp. ground turmeric
giblets from chicken
2 tbsp. currants
about 10 fl. oz (300 ml) chicken
    stock
3 cucumbers
1 tsp. lemon juice
1 tbsp. flour
3 tbsp. milk
seasoning

Cut chickens into large pieces. Heat oil in large pan, stir in curry powder.
Brown chicken pieces in hot oil. Add finely chopped onions, peeled and sliced
ginger, garlic, peppers, ground ginger and turmeric. Chop giblets finely,
add to pan with currants, and sufficient chicken stock to cover. Simmer until
meat starts to fall from the bones. Remove chicken and skin; cut meat into
serving pieces. Cut scrubbed, unpeeled cucumbers into 1 in. (2 cm) pieces,
add to sauce with lemon juice. Simmer gently until cucumbers are tender.
Strain liquid into small pan, add flour combined with milk; cook, stirring,
until thickened. Return to large saucepan, together with chicken pieces and
cucumber. Simmer gently, covered, additional 5 minutes, adding a little
more milk if sauce is too thick. Season to taste. Serve with rice. *Serves 6.*

CHICKEN CURRY

1 medium-size chicken (about 3 lb
    (1·35 kg))
2 medium onions, finely sliced
2 oz (50 g) butter
4 tbsp. water
1 dessp. coconut cream, softened
    in 2 tbsp. hot water (p. 13)

2 tomatoes, skinned and chopped
salt
5 tbsp. infusion of tamarind (or
    1 tbsp. redcurrant jelly, mixed
    with the juice of ½ lemon in
    4 tbsp. water) (p. 13)
1 tbsp. ground almonds

Spice paste:
1 tbsp. ground coriander
½ tsp. fenugreek
1 tsp. chilli powder
½ tsp. ground ginger

1½ tsp. cumin seed
½ tsp. ground turmeric
1 clove garlic (crushed with salt)
½ tsp. garam masala (p. 13)

Mix all the spices to paste with a little water. Joint chicken. Fry onions until
brown in butter. Stir in spice paste and fry gently 2 minutes. Add chicken and
cook 3–4 minutes, turning it over once. Pour in water, coconut milk, and add
chopped tomatoes and 1 teaspoon salt. Cover and cook gently until chicken
is tender. Add infusion of tamarind. Mix ground almonds with a little water
to moisten and stir them in. Remove lid to reduce liquid if necessary and
taste for seasoning. *Serves 4–6.*

CHICKEN IN A POT

2 lb (900 g) chicken
½ tsp. chilli powder
½ tsp. ground ginger
4 oz (100 g) long-grain rice
4 tbsp. green pepper, chopped
2 tomatoes, chopped
4 oz (100 g) button mushrooms, halved

6 tbsp. butter
salt
4 mint leaves
4 onions, sliced
3 tsp. ground turmeric
2 tbsp. ground coriander
1 tsp. ground cumin

Wash chicken well and dry. Prick it all over with a fork and rub in chilli and powdered ginger. Boil rice. Drain and mix with pepper, tomatoes, mushrooms, 1 tablespoon butter, salt to taste and bruised mint leaves. Stuff chicken with this. Heat remaining butter, brown onions, then add turmeric, coriander and cumin, and fry gently for 2 minutes. Brown chicken on all sides, mixing it well with spices and onions. Transfer to a casserole dish with all gravy. Sprinkle salt and more turmeric over, add ¼ pint (150 ml) water. Close lid tightly and bake at 300°F (150°C), Gas Mark 2, for about 1½ hours until cooked. Add more liquid if necessary. Uncover for last 5 minutes, raising the heat to 425°F (220°C), Gas Mark 7.

CHICKEN PAPRIKA

3 lb (1·5 kg) chicken
2 oz (50 g) flour
2 tsp. mixed seasoning
1½ tbsp. paprika
¼ tsp. black pepper
½ tsp. ground ginger
¼ tsp. garlic powder
¼ tsp. basil leaves

dash nutmeg
2 tbsp. butter or margarine
2 tbsp. cooking fat
4 tbsp. sherry or water
2 tsp. Worcestershire sauce
½ chicken stock cube
4 oz (100 g) tin mushrooms
10 fl. oz (300 ml) sour cream

Cut chicken in pieces, coat with mixture of flour, mixed seasoning, paprika, pepper, ginger, garlic powder, basil leaves and nutmeg. Heat butter and fat in heavy pan. Brown chicken slowly. Combine sherry, Worcester sauce and stock cube, pour over browned chicken. Add mushrooms. Cover and simmer 45 minutes or until tender. Remove chicken to serving platter. Blend sour cream with dripping in pan, stir 2 to 3 minutes until sour cream is heated but do not allow to boil. Pour sauce over chicken, sprinkle with additional paprika. *Serves 4.*

CHICKEN TERI-YAKI

3 lb (1·35 kg) chicken cut into 8 pieces
6½ fl. oz (180 ml) soy sauce
2 tbsp. sugar

1 clove garlic, chopped
2½ fl. oz (75 ml) sake or white wine
½ tsp. ground ginger

Combine all ingredients except chicken to make marinade. Place chicken in the marinade for 1 hour. Bake in moderate oven 350°F (180°C), Gas Mark 4, 1 hour or until chicken is cooked. Baste 2 or 3 times while cooking. *Serves 4–6.*

GLAZED GOOSE WITH APPLES,
GINGER AND GREEN PEPPERS

1 goose
salt and black pepper
4 large cloves garlic
1 green pepper, deseeded
8 oz (225 g) chopped preserved
   ginger
1½ lb (675 g) eating apples

juice of 1 lemon
4 fl. oz (125 ml) natural yoghurt
5 fl. oz (150 ml) apple juice
2 tbsp. caster sugar
2 tbsp. soya sauce
a handful of fresh coriander, mint
   or parsley, chopped

Remove the giblets and lumps of fat from inside the goose. Rub the skin with salt and place the goose breast side down on a rack in a large roasting tin. Place the pieces of goose fat on top and cover the tin with foil. Preheat the oven to 350°F (180°C), Gas Mark 4, and roast the goose for 20 minutes per lb (450 g).

While the goose is cooking chop finely together the garlic, ginger and deseeded green pepper. Peel and slice the apples.

Put 5 tbsp. of goose fat from the roasting tin into a saucepan with the chopped garlic, ginger and green pepper mixture and heat over medium heat for 1 minute. Then add the sliced apples, stir and cover the saucepan. Cook over a low heat for 10 minutes and then add the lemon juice and seasoning. Cover and cook until the apples are fairly mushy, stir in the yoghurt and remove from heat.

About 45 minutes before the goose has finished cooking remove as much fat as possible from the roasting tin and pour in the apple juice. Turn the goose breast side up and brush with a mixture of caster sugar and soya sauce. Continue to cook uncovered. When ready to serve, reheat the apple mixture and stir in the chopped coriander, mint or parsley leaves. Spoon the apple mixture on top of the cooked carved goose when serving. *Serves 6–8.*

CHIHOMBILY

3½ lb (1·5 kg) chicken
seasoning to taste
dash garlic salt
dash celery salt
1 tbsp. sherry
oil for frying
1 2 in. (5 cm) piece of fresh ginger
2 onions, finely chopped

3 tbsp. tomato paste
1 tbsp. flour
5 fl. oz (150 ml) chicken stock
small tin mushrooms
2 large tomatoes
1 clove garlic
dash OK sauce
8 oz (225 g) frozen peas

Cut up chicken for frying. Season with salt, pepper, garlic salt, celery salt and sherry, put aside. Heat oil and fry ginger until brown and discard. Add chicken, fry until brown and remove from pan. Fry onions, add chicken. Add tomato paste, a little flour and stock, mushrooms, tomatoes, clove of garlic cut very small and a dash of OK sauce. Cook together slowly until chicken is tender. Add peas 10 minutes before serving. *Serves 4.*

DUCKLING À L'ORANGE

3 lb (1½ kg) duckling
1 tsp. salt
¼ tsp. black pepper
4 tbsp. orange juice
8 oz (225 g) brown sugar
4 tsp. orange peel, grated

½ tsp. dry mustard
¼ tsp. allspice
¼ tsp. ginger
2 tbsp. flour
20 fl. oz (600 ml) orange juice

Clean duckling. Rub inside and outside with salt and pepper. Place on rack in roasting pan, breast side down. Roast at 450°F (230°C), Gas Mark 8, for 30 minutes. Reduce temperature to 350°F (180°C), Gas Mark 4, and turn duckling so breast side is up. Continue roasting, allowing 30 minutes per pound (500 g). The last 30 minutes of cooking time begin basting with mixture: 2 tablespoons orange juice, brown sugar, 3 teaspoons of the orange peel, dry mustard, allspice and ginger. Continue basting with dripping from pan until duckling is tender and skin is crisp and brown. Remove to plate and keep hot. Pour off grease. Stir flour and remaining 1 teaspoon orange peel into pan dripping. Add rest of orange juice and cook over low heat until thickened, stirring constantly. Strain liquid into sauce dish and serve with hot duckling. *Serves 3.*

FAIRY DUCK

1 fat duck (4–4½ lb, 1¾–2 kg)
salt and pepper
2 pieces ginger
½ tsp. minced ginger

2 tbsp. wine
2 stalks spring onions
2 oz (50 g) cooked ham slices
2 oz (50 g) bamboo shoots, sliced

Clean duck; rub with salt, pepper, wine and minced ginger and let this stand for 1 hour in earthenware casserole. Transfer to a saucepan, add spring onions and ginger pieces and cover with water. Allow to boil and then simmer for 4 hours steadily. Add ham and bamboo shoots 10 minutes before serving. *Serves 4.*

CHINESE DUCK

4–5 lb (1¾–2¼ kg) duck
1 clove garlic
oil (for browning)

Sauce:
4 tbsp. soy sauce
1 dessp. vinegar
1 tbsp. ginger (finely chopped)

15 oz (425 g) tin pineapple slices
10 fl. oz (300 ml) stock made from
    giblets
1 dessp. cornflour
1 tbsp. sugar
1 tsp. sherry

Rub duck with garlic; heat oil in large pan or flameproof casserole and brown duck all over. Pour off any surplus oil, drain pineapple slices and add juice and stock to pan. Cover and cook gently for about 1 hour. Combine sauce ingredients in bowl. Grill duck to crisp the skin. Strain juices from the stewpan, skim and add the sauce. Boil up well and thicken with a little cornflour. Spoon sauce over and around duck and surround with the sliced pineapple browned in a little duck fat if wished. Serve with fried rice. *Serves 4.*

MANDARIN DUCKLING

4–5 lb (1¾–2¼ kg) duckling
2 tbsp. honey
1 tsp. soy sauce
10 oz (275 g) tin mandarin
    oranges
15 oz (425 g) tin pineapple cubes

3 tbsp. cornflour
3 tbsp. soy sauce
2 tbsp. sherry
¼ tsp. ground ginger
1 green pepper ⎱ seeded and
1 red pepper ⎰ diced

Stuffing:
2 large onions, chopped
8 oz (225 g) tin celery,
    drained and chopped
1 tbsp. soy sauce
1 tbsp. dry sherry

1 tbsp. sugar
1 tsp. salt
½ tsp. ground cinnamon
½ tsp. ground ginger

Wash duckling and dry thoroughly. Score skin all over at 1 in. intervals. Skewer neck skin to back. Combine the ingredients for stuffing and pour inside duckling, sew cavity closed, bring legs together and tie. Place on rack in shallow roasting pan, roast at 325°F (170°C), Gas Mark 3, for about 2½ hours.

When cooked, remove from oven and pour off juices and fat from pan. Mix honey and soy sauce together, spread all over duckling. Replace in oven 500°F (250°C), Gas Mark 9–10, for 15–20 minutes, basting frequently with glaze.

Drain oranges and pineapple. Add enough water to juice to make 20 fl. oz (600 ml). Blend cornflour with cold juice, add to remainder of liquid together with soy sauce, ginger and sherry. Cook till sauce thickens, stirring constantly. Add orange segments, pineapple cubes and diced peppers, simmer for 5–10 minutes.

To serve: divide duckling into joints but place together again, tucking segments of fruit into cuts to hide them, pour sauce containing fruit all around duckling. *Serves 4–6.*

PINEAPPLE CHICKEN

2½ lb (1.25 kg) chicken pieces
2 tsp. cooking oil
1 onion, chopped
1 clove garlic, crushed
4 oz (100 g) chopped preserved
   ginger
10 fl. oz (300 ml) unsweetened
   pineapple juice

1 tbsp. cornflour
2 chicken stock cubes
10 fl. oz (300 ml) hot water
2 tsp. soya sauce
salt and pepper
1 tbsp. dry sherry

Heat the oil in a large pan and gently fry the chicken and onion until golden brown. Remove and drain off the oil, add the crushed garlic and ginger, and sauté gently for 1 minute. Add the pineapple juice combined with the cornflour, chicken stock cubes dissolved in the water, and all the other ingredients except the sherry, and gently heat while stirring continuously until the sauce boils and thickens.

Return the chicken to the pan and stir gently into the sauce. Cover and simmer gently for about 30 minutes until the chicken is cooked, add sherry and cook for another minute or so. Serve right away. *Serves 6.*

EGGS IN PINEAPPLE SAUCE

6 hard-boiled eggs

4–6 portions boiled rice

Sauce:
2 onions, chopped
1 tbsp. oil
12 oz (350 g) tin pineapple cubes
1 level tbsp. cornflour

2 tsp. vinegar
2 tomatoes, chopped
¼ tbsp. ground ginger
salt and pepper to taste

Fry onions in oil till brown. Drain pineapple, reserving syrup. Blend cornflour with some of the syrup; break up pineapple cubes. Add cornflour paste, rest of syrup, pineapple and vinegar to onions, stirring as sauce thickens. Add tomatoes, ginger, salt and pepper. Simmer for 10 minutes. Place halved eggs on bed of rice, pour sauce over. *Serves 4–6.*

SIMPLE EGG CURRY

4 hard-boiled eggs
2 oz (50 g) butter
1 large onion, finely sliced
2 tsp. curry powder (p. 13)
¼ tsp. ground ginger

¼ green pepper, seeded and
   chopped
salt
10 fl. oz (300 ml) water
1 tbsp. lemon juice

Shell and halve eggs. Heat butter and fry onion until lightly browned. Add spices and cook gently for 1–2 minutes. Stir in chopped green pepper and ¼ tsp. salt. Blend in water and stir until sauce has thickened. Add lemon juice and put in eggs, cut surface down. Spoon sauce over them and leave for about 10 minutes for the eggs to heat through before serving. *Serves 4.*

4
Fish

This brief section contains an interesting collection of ginger recipes for fish and shellfish. Using ginger with fish is one of the most original ways of adding flavour that is different.

BASS WITH GINGER

1½–2 lb (700–900 g) bass
water
salt
1 dessp. soy sauce

1 tsp. oil
1 tsp. ground ginger or 1 tbsp.
    finely chopped fresh ginger
2 oz (50 g) chopped spring onions

Place fish in plenty of boiling, salted water. Bring to boil again, then cook gently 5 minutes until done. Drain fish carefully and arrange on serving dish. Combine soy sauce, oil and ginger, pour over fish, garnish with spring onions and serve. Fresh ginger is preferable to ground ginger. *Serves 4–6.*

CHINESE FRIED HADDOCK

1 lb (450 g) haddock
salt
1 dessp. brandy
1–2 oz (25–50 g) oil

2 cloves garlic
1 slice green ginger
4–5 spring onions
1 tbsp. vinegar

Sprinkle fish with salt and brandy and leave for several hours, if possible overnight. Cut into collops and fry in very hot oil until golden. Pound garlic and ginger into paste, add chopped spring onions, blend with vinegar, sprinkle over fish and serve. *Serves 4.*

FLOUNDER IN GINGER

6 flounder (or small sole) fillets
3 tbsp. plain flour
1 tbsp. ground ginger
3 eggs

1 tbsp. soy sauce
3 tbsp. chopped spring onion
3 tbsp. sherry

Sift flour and ginger into bowl. Beat eggs, soy sauce, onion and sherry all together. Add egg mixture to dry ingredients, gradually, beating well with wooden spoon. Cut flounder fillets into strips, dip into batter and fry in deep hot oil until golden and crisp. *Serves 6.*

SWEET AND SOUR MULLET

1 large or 2 small mullet, filleted	2 tbsp. vinegar
seasoning	1 tbsp. brown sugar
1 tbsp. cornflour	4 thin slices green ginger
15 fl. oz (400 ml) water	2 tbsp. diced pineapple
1 dessp. soy sauce	chopped shallots

Wash, dry and season fish. Arrange in greased casserole. Blend cornflour with a little water. Place water, soy sauce, vinegar, sugar and cornflour mixture in saucepan and stir over gentle heat until thickened. Add finely chopped ginger, pineapple and shallots. Spoon sauce over fish, reserving about 4 tbsp. Cover dish and bake at 350°F (180°C), Gas Mark 4, 25 minutes or until fish is tender and flakes when tested with fork. Serve with sauce. *Serves 4.*

TUNA WITH GINGER RICE

15 oz (425 g) tin tuna	8 oz (225 g) sliced celery
1 tbsp. cornflour	8 oz (225 g) sliced french beans
12½ fl. oz (375 ml) water	½ tsp. salt
1 medium onion, chopped	1 tsp. sugar
2 oz (50 g) butter	1 tsp. soy sauce

Ginger rice:
3 cups cooked rice	1 tsp. ground ginger

Blend cornflour with a little water. Fry onion in butter until tender. Add celery, french beans, salt and remaining water. Bring to boil, cover and simmer for 5 minutes. Add cornflour, sugar and soy sauce and cook for 3 minutes longer, stirring constantly. Add tuna in chunks, undrained, and reheat. Serve over hot rice spiced with ground ginger. *Serves 2–3.*

CRAB CAKES

1 lb (450 g) crab meat	¼ tsp. ginger
2 slices bread, in crumbs	freshly-ground pepper
1 egg, lightly beaten	1 tbsp. Worcestershire sauce
1 tbsp. mayonnaise	⅛ tsp. cayenne
1 tsp. parsley flakes	1 tbsp. baking powder
1½ tsp. celery salt	dash cloves
¼ tsp. dry mustard	cooking oil for deep frying

Mix breadcrumbs with egg. Add mayonnaise, parsley flakes, celery salt, dry mustard, ginger, pepper, Worcester sauce, cayenne, baking powder and cloves. Mix thoroughly then combine with crab meat. Shape into 8 cakes. Fry in deep fat at 375°F (190°C) for 4 minutes or until golden brown. *Serves 4.*

ORIENTAL FISH

8 oz (225 g) plaice fillets
6 pieces preserved ginger

4 oz (100 g) prawns
a little melted butter

Marinade
2 tbsp. oil

2 tbsp. clear honey

Remove the skin from the plaice fillets. Mix the honey and oil together. Put the plaice in a non-metallic dish, pour the marinade over and leave for 1 hour. Cut the plaice into strips.

Cut the ginger into smaller pieces. Thread the prawns, plaice and ginger onto six skewers, brush with a little melted butter and then place under a moderately hot grill. Cook for 6–10 minutes until the plaice is cooked but not browning. Turn the kebabs about 3 times whilst grilling. *Makes 6 kebabs.*

GINGERED SOLE

1½ lb (700 g) fillets of sole (or plaice)
8 oz (225 g) cooked prawns or
shrimps
8 fl. oz (250 ml) chicken stock
2½ fl. oz (75 ml) white wine

2 tbsp. chopped preserved ginger
2 tsp. lime juice
1 tbsp. cornflour
1 tbsp. water
1 tsp. butter or margarine

Roll the sole (or plaice) fillets around the prawns and secure each with a toothpick. In a saucepan, bring the chicken stock, wine, ginger and lime juice to a simmer. Add the fish fillets, cover and continue to simmer gently for about 5 minutes until the fish flakes.

Transfer the fish to a heated serving dish and remove the toothpicks. Mix the cornflour and water and add to the stock, stirring over a gentle heat until it thickens. Stir in the butter and serve over the fish. *Serves 4.*

GINGERY SEAFOOD

One of the interesting ways to deal with fish such as cod, whiting or haddock is to marinade it first in a mixture of lemon and ginger.

1½ lb (700 g) cod, whiting or
haddock
4 oz (100 g) finely chopped
preserved ginger

salt
juice of 2 lemons

Place the fish in a shallow dish and cover with the chopped preserved ginger, a sprinkling of salt and the lemon juice. Marinade for at least 1 hour. The fish can either be baked in its marinade with a knob of butter and a glass of white wine, covered with foil, or dried, floured and fried until crisp. Garlic can be added to the marinade if desired. *Serves 6.*

PRAWNS CREOLE

1 lb (450 g) prawns
1 tbsp. oil
1 onion, sliced
1 clove of garlic
4 oz (100 g) tin mushrooms
½ red pepper, sliced
1 stick celery, chopped

½ in. (1 cm) piece green ginger
4 oz (100 g) cashew nuts
salt
pinch of cayenne
1 tsp. Worcestershire sauce
5 fl. oz (150 ml) cream

Shell prawns. Heat oil in heavy pan. Add onion, sauté with garlic until onion is soft and golden. Add mushrooms, pepper and celery. Remove garlic, add ginger, cashews, salt and cayenne. Cook gently 10 minutes. Add prawns, Worcester sauce and cream. Heat through gently, do not boil. Serve with hot boiled rice. *Serves 3.*

PRAWNS WITH ALMONDS

1 lb (450 g) large prawns
4 oz (100 g) blanched almonds
salt
1 tsp. ground ginger
1 dessp. cornflour
1 tbsp. oil

1 clove chopped garlic
pepper
2 oz (50 g) finely chopped celery
1 tsp. soy sauce
1 tsp. brandy
2 tbsp. water

Toss almonds in slightly greased frying pan with salt, just enough to turn them light golden. Be careful not to burn. Drain on greaseproof paper. Peel prawns, leaving tail tips on. Split prawns lengthwise and remove intestinal cord. Sprinkle with salt, put in basin, add ginger and cornflour and mix well. Heat oil in pan, add garlic, cook for 1 minute, then remove garlic. Put in prawns and cook for 3 minutes, stirring constantly. Season with pepper, add celery, and cook for 4 more minutes. Add soy sauce and brandy. Rinse basin in which the prawns were mixed with the water and pour contents into pan. Bring to boil. Add almonds, stir, allow to come to boil once more, and serve. *Serves 4–6.*

BRANDIED SCALLOPS

8 oz (225 g) scallops
8 oz (225 g) green pepper, chopped
1 tsp. cornflour
5 fl. oz (150 ml) water
1 dessp. soy sauce

1 tbsp. oil
1 tsp. minced green ginger
2 cloves garlic, crushed
salt and pepper
1 dessp. brandy

Cut green pepper into small dice. Mix cornflour with water and add soy sauce. Heat oil in pan with ginger and garlic and fry scallops for 4 minutes, seasoning well. Add pepper and cook for 3 or 4 minutes. Pour in soy and cornflour mixture, bring to boil. Light brandy and immediately pour into pan. Blend and serve at once. *Serves 4.*

SHRIMP CURRY

3 lb (1·35 kg) shrimps
2 oz (50 g) finely chopped onion
1 tbsp. finely chopped shallot
4 oz (100 g) butter
4 oz (100 g) flour

2 tbsp. curry powder (p. 13)
20 fl. oz (600 ml) coconut juice
20 fl. oz (600 ml) milk
2 tsp. ground ginger
3 tbsp. lemon juice

Shell and wash shrimps with salty water. Sauté onion, shallot in butter in large saucepan for 5 minutes. Stir in flour and curry powder. Add coconut juice and fresh milk and cook over low heat until thickened, stirring constantly. Add shrimps, ginger, lemon juice and some salt. Simmer uncovered for 20 minutes stirring frequently. *Serves 6.*

SPICED FRIED PRAWNS

1 lb (450 g) shelled prawns
3 tsp. coriander
pinch powdered ginger
2 tsp. sugar
¼ tsp. salt

½ tsp. black pepper
2 tsp. vinegar
2 cloves garlic, crushed
oil for deep frying

Combine all ingredients except prawns and oil. Coat prawns with mixture, leave for 3 hours. Deep fry in hot oil, drain on absorbent paper. Serve hot. *Serves 6.*

SALMON IN PASTRY WITH GINGER

1¾ lb (800 g) middle cut of salmon
3 tbsp. sunflower or walnut oil
1 tbsp. lemon juice
2 tbsp. dry white wine
salt and pepper

14 oz (400 g) puff pastry
beaten egg
3 large pieces preserved ginger
  in syrup
2 oz (50 g) raisins

Split the salmon in half, remove all the bones and skin, then divide the two pieces lengthways to give 4 fillets.

Put the fillets in a dish with the oil, lemon juice, white wine and pepper. Allow to marinade for about 6 hours, turning occasionally, then drain. Divide the pastry into 2 pieces, one a little larger than the other. Roll both out into rectangles.

Brush the smaller piece of pastry with beaten egg and on top of this lay 2 of the salmon fillets. Season them with salt and pepper, then cover with fine slices of ginger and the raisins soaked in a little hot water. Cover this with the remaining two fillets of salmon and season again. Lay the second piece of pastry over all, seal the edges and trim into an attractive shape.

Brush the top of the pastry parcel with beaten egg, decorate and make a few holes to allow the steam to escape. Cook in a preheated oven at 375°F (190°C), Gas Mark 5, for 35–40 minutes. Serve very hot with Hollandaise sauce. *Serves 6.*

5
Vegetable dishes and salads

Use ginger in its various forms to gave flavour to special dressings. Chopped ginger especially adds piquancy to salad and vegetable dishes.

CITRUS LETTUCE SALAD

1 large lettuce
½ bunch watercress
1 grapefruit, sectioned
2 oranges, sectioned
12 dates, stoned

2 oz (50 g) chopped preserved ginger
1 tbsp. French dressing made with lemon juice, oil, salt and pepper
3 oz (75 g) cream cheese

Tear lettuce and watercress into bite-size pieces in salad bowl. Add grapefruit and orange, dates, ginger and just enough French dressing to moisten slightly. Crumble cream cheese into salad and toss lightly. *Serves 4.*

CREAMY COLESLAW

5 fl. oz (150 ml) sour cream
1 tbsp. vinegar
1 tsp. mixed seasoning
1½ tbsp. sugar
½ tsp. dry mustard
¼ tsp. ground ginger

½ tsp. celery salt
dash white pepper
1½–2 lb (675–900g) finely shredded white cabbage
3 oz (75 g) minced green pepper
paprika

Combine sour cream with the next seven ingredients. Refrigerate 20 minutes, allowing seasonings to blend. Spoon over cabbage and green pepper, tossing lightly. Sprinkle with paprika. *Serves 4-6.*

PEACH AND GINGER SALAD

1 lettuce
3 tbsp. preserved ginger, sliced
juice of ½ lemon
2 tbsp. olive oil
3 fresh peaches

salt
pepper, freshly ground
1 tbsp. ginger syrup
chopped parsley to garnish

Trim and wash lettuce, remove heart. Dry lettuce thoroughly, then open it out. Scald, skin and slice peaches (after removing stones), mix with ginger and spoon into centre of lettuce. Arrange this on serving dish. Mix seasoning with lemon juice and ginger syrup and whisk in oil until mixture thickens. Spoon this over fruit and dust with a little chopped parsley. *Serves 4.*

PEAR MANGO SALAD

1 small fresh pineapple
8 oz (225 g) creamed cottage cheese
2 pears, peeled and cut in chunks
1 mango, peeled and sliced

1½ tbsp. toasted, sliced Brazil nuts
1½ tbsp. sliced preserved ginger
sweet French dressing

Beginning at crown, cut pineapple in half lengthways. Scoop out fruit. In bottom of each half, place layer of cottage cheese. Remove core from pineapple and cut fruit into chunks. Place layer over the cottage cheese. Arrange a layer each of pears and mangoes over the pineapple. Top with a sprinkling of ginger and nuts, and serve with a sweet French dressing. *Serves 4.*

MASHED TURNIPS WITH GINGER

2½ lb (1.25 kg) turnips
4 oz (100 g) butter

4 oz (100 g) finely chopped
  preserved ginger
salt and pepper

Peel, cut up and cook the turnips in salted water for about 10 minutes until soft; drain. Melt the butter in a pan and fry the ginger for minute or two. Pour over the cooked turnips and mash well, seasoning to taste. Serve while hot. *Serves 6–8.*

CARROT AND GREEN PEPPER SALAD

1 oz (25 g) sultanas
8 oz (225 g) carrots, peeled and
  grated coarsely
1 large green pepper, deseeded and
  chopped

2 tbsp. oil
1 tbsp. lemon juice or vinegar
1 tsp. salt
black pepper
2 oz (50 g) chopped preserved ginger

In a bowl toss together well the sultanas, carrot and green pepper in the oil, lemon juice or vinegar, salt, pepper and the ginger. *Serves 4.*

GINGERED POTATOES WITH SPINACH

1 lb (450 g) peeled potatoes
8 oz (225 g) frozen spinach
2 oz (50 g) finely chopped preserved
  ginger

a little oil
salt

Pour a thin film of oil into a saucepan with a tight-fitting lid. Cut the potatoes into 1–2-in. (2.5–5-cm) pieces. Add all the other ingredients to the heated oil in the pan and cover. Steam gently, giving the pan an occasional shake to prevent sticking and ensure that all is cooked through, for about 15–20 minutes. Serve with curries or kebabs. *Serves 4.*

CHINESE GINGER SALAD

1 large tomato
1 carrot
1 banana
2 pineapple rings
2 sticks celery
1 apple
½ cucumber

1 lettuce heart
2 tbsp. oil
2 tbsp. cider vinegar
2 oz (50 g) finely chopped
    crystallized ginger
1 oz (25 g) chopped walnuts

Cut into pieces the tomato, carrot, banana, pineapple, celery, apple, cucumber and lettuce and place in a salad bowl. Mix together the oil and vinegar, ginger and walnuts to make a dressing, pour over the salad ingredients in the bowl and toss well. *Serves 4-6.*

CURRIED CAULIFLOWER

1 large cauliflower
10 fl. oz (300 ml) yoghurt
1 onion, grated
2 cloves garlic, crushed
1 tsp. ground ginger
1 tsp. sugar
2 oz (50 g) butter

2 onions, coarsely chopped
1 tsp. salt
15 fl. oz (400 ml) hot water
½ tsp. ground cinnamon
¼ tsp. ground nutmeg
¼ tsp. ground coriander

Separate cauliflower into florets and rinse. Put yoghurt in large bowl and add grated onion, garlic, ginger and sugar. Add florets and let stand for 2 hours, turning pieces several times. Heat butter in large pan and brown onions in it; add cauliflower with yoghurt dressing. Add salt and water and simmer for about 20 minutes, till vegetable is tender but not mushy. Most of liquid should be absorbed and only a small amount of the thick sauce should remain. Remove from heat and sprinkle with mixed cinnamon, nutmeg and coriander. *Serves 4.*

CURRIED POTATO CAKES

8 oz (225 g) cold mashed potato
8 oz (225 g) cooked green peas
1 tbsp. green chillis, chopped
good pinch ground ginger

good pinch ground coriander
salt to taste
1 egg, beaten
4 oz (100 g) butter or vegetable oil

Mix potato, peas, chillis, ginger and coriander together. Add salt to taste. Form into small flat cakes. Dip in beaten egg, and fry in hot butter or oil until well browned. *Serves 3-4.*

FRESH GINGERED CARROTS

1 tbsp. fresh lemon juice
1 tsp. salt
¾ tsp. ground ginger
⅛ tsp ground black pepper

1½ lb (675 g) cooked fresh carrots,
    sliced
butter

Combine lemon juice, salt, ground ginger and pepper. Sprinkle over carrots.
Dot with butter and bake in preheated oven 400°F (200°C), Gas Mark 6,
45 minutes. *Serves 4.*

GINGERED CUCUMBERS

2 cucumbers
1 tsp. salt
4 tbsp. white vinegar

1 tsp. green ginger
1½ tbsp. sugar

Peel cucumbers, score with fork, cut into thin slices. Place in bowl, sprinkle
with salt, set aside 30 minutes. Drain off excess liquid. Finely chop ginger
and mix with remaining ingredients, add to cucumbers, mix well. Refrigerate
well before serving. *Serves 4.*

GINGER SWEET POTATOES

4 medium-size sweet potatoes
salt and pepper
2–3 tbsp. butter or margarine
3 oz (75 g) sugar

4 tbsp. water
2 tbsp. honey
¾ tsp. ground ginger
4 tbsp. fresh orange juice

Peel, slice and cook potatoes. Arrange in buttered casserole, sprinkling each
layer with pinch each salt, ground black pepper, and 1 tbsp. butter or margarine. Mix rest of ingredients and pour over potatoes. Bake 30 minutes or
until glazed, 350°F (180°C), Gas Mark 4. *Serves 4.*

GINGER GLAZED CARROTS

1 bunch carrots
1 chicken stock cube
1 tsp. sugar
7½ fl. oz (225 ml) water
4 tbsp. butter

1 tbsp. lemon juice
3 tbsp. honey
½ tsp. ginger
½ tsp. nutmeg
parsley flakes

Clean carrots and cut into rounds. Put in skillet with stock cube, sugar,
water and 1 tbsp. butter. Cover; cook 12 minutes; drain. Add remaining
butter, lemon juice, honey, ginger and nutmeg. Cook, uncovered, over medium heat 2–3 minutes, tossing frequently to glaze carrots thoroughly. Sprinkle
with parsley flakes before serving. *Serves 4.*

Shami kebabs with, in the background, Indonesian chicken and citrus
lettuce salad

Ginger pear flan

Overleaf: CLOCKWISE FROM TOP LEFT: gingerbread men, ginger chips, ginger fruit cake, ginger ice cream, honey-glazed pork shoulder, ginger wine, duckling à l'orange (with its accompanying sauce in the gravy boat), ginger bombe, ginger cream, ginger and melon coronets

INDIAN BEAN FOOGATH

8 oz (225 g) runner beans
5 fl. oz (150 ml) water
salt
4 small onions
2 tbsp. butter

½ in. (1 cm) piece green ginger
½ tsp. ground turmeric
4 cloves garlic
2 green chillis
1 tbsp. desiccated coconut

Wash and string beans, chop finely. Place in pan with water, salt to taste, and two of onions, finely chopped. Boil until soft, simmer until all water evaporates, remove from heat. Slice remaining onions and brown in another pan in butter, add ginger, turmeric, garlic, chillis and beans. Stir 3 minutes, then remove. Add coconut, return to heat for 1 or 2 minutes. *Serves 2-3.*

PURÉE OF SWEDE

2 lb (900 g) swede
1 lb (450 g) potatoes
1 stock cube

½ tsp. ground ginger
about 10 fl. oz (300 ml) hot water

Wash, peel and dice swede and potatoes. Dissolve stock cube in hot water. Place diced vegetables in saucepan and pour stock over. There should be just enough for vegetables to simmer without burning. When soft, mash into stock, which should be reduced if necessary to make right consistency of purée. Mix in ginger and serve. *Serves 6-8.*

VEGETARIAN RICE

7 oz (200 g) brown rice
1 tbsp. oil
2 large onions
4 cloves garlic
1 oz (25 g) fresh ginger
1 oz (25 g) blanched halved almonds
2 sticks celery, chopped

8 shallots, chopped
½ red or green pepper, deseeded
  and chopped
2 oz (50 g) mushrooms, sliced
3 oz (75 g) sultanas
2 tbsp. chopped parsley
salt

Cook the rice in a large saucepan of boiling salted water for 25–30 minutes or until just tender; drain well. Peel and chop the onions, crush the garlic, peel and grate the ginger.

Heat the oil in a wok or large frying pan, add the garlic, onion and ginger, and cook until the onion is transparent. Add the almonds and cook a further 2 minutes, turning constantly. Add the rice, mix well, then add the chopped celery, shallots, pepper, sliced mushrooms and sultanas. Season with salt. Cook, uncovered, for a further 3 minutes or until well combined and heated through. Add the chopped parsley and toss well. *Serves 4.*

6
Desserts and ice-creams

Ginger ice-cream is a popular choice everywhere. In Britain, steamed ginger pudding is a traditionally warming dish for cold winter days. As well as these favourites, this collection includes all sorts of sweet recipes from many parts of the world.

GINGERED GRAPE AND PEAR MOULD

10 fl. oz (300 ml) hot water
3 oz (75 g) packaged lemon jelly
10 fl. oz (300 ml) ginger ale
2–3 diced fresh pears
3 oz (75 g) halved seeded grapes

1 oz (25 g) chopped walnuts
2 tsp. finely chopped crystallized
   ginger
salad greens
mayonnaise or other salad dressing

Pour hot water over jelly, stir until dissolved. Cool. Stir in ginger ale and chill until syrupy. Mix together the pears, grapes, nuts and ginger and stir into the jelly mixture. Turn into a one-quart (one-litre) ring mould or six individual moulds. Chill until firm. Unmould on salad greens. Serve with a bowl of mayonnaise in the centre of the ring. *Serves 6.*

GINGER CANDY

1 lb (450 g) soft brown sugar
5 fl. oz (150 ml) water
2 oz (50 g) golden syrup

2 level tsp. ground ginger
1 oz (25 g) butter

Grease a tin 8 inches (20 cm) square. Put all ingredients into large heavy saucepan. Heat slowly, stirring all the time until sugar dissolves and butter melts. Bring to boil and cover with lid. Boil 2 minutes, then uncover. Continue to boil steadily, stirring once or twice, until a little of the mixture forms a soft ball when dropped into cold water. Cool 5 minutes then beat briskly until mixture becomes cloudy. Spread into prepared tin and cut into squares when cold and set.

CHOCOLATE GINGERBALLS

4 oz (100 g) cooking chocolate
1½ oz (37 g) crystallized ginger

When chocolate has just melted, stir in ginger, cut into very thin shreds. Stir lightly until blended, then with two teaspoons take out small portions of mixture. Place on greaseproof paper. Leave to harden.

GINGER CREAM

2–3 oz (50–75 g) preserved ginger
10 fl. oz (300 ml) milk
3 egg yolks
caster sugar to taste

½ oz (12 g) gelatine
4 tbsp. water
2–3 tbsp. ginger syrup
10 fl. oz (300 ml) double cream

Infuse chopped preserved ginger in milk. Beat eggs and sugar until liquid and make thick pouring custard with flavoured milk. Strain. Allow to cool and thicken. Soak gelatine in water for 5 minutes then heat to dissolve. Stir ginger syrup gently into cooled custard, add dissolved gelatine, stirring again as it cools. Whip cream and fold lightly into custard mixture just before setting. Pour into a prepared mould or into glass dishes. *Serves 6.*

GINGER MOULD

15 oz (425 g) tin evaporated milk
5 fl. oz (150 ml) vanilla custard
1 oz (25 g) gelatine
3 tbsp. preserved ginger syrup

2 oz (50 g) caster sugar
1 little lemon jelly
2 oz (50 g) preserved ginger

Beat chilled evaporated milk and fold in cold custard. Dissolve gelatine in water and add ginger syrup and sugar. Add to custard mixture with chopped preserved ginger. As mixture is setting, pour into wetted mould and allow to set. Turn on to plate and decorate with chopped lemon jelly. *Serves 4.*

GINGER FROSTING FOR CAKES AND SPONGES

Stir 1 dessertspoon lemon juice into ½ cup condensed milk until mixture thickens, then gradually add 1 cup icing sugar, ½ teaspoon ground ginger and ½ cup preserved ginger shredded very finely. Pile thickly on cakes and decorate with small pieces of ginger.

GINGER PEAR MELBA

1 Cornish ice-cream
1 tbsp. green ginger wine
½ oz (12 g) roasted flaked almonds

1 or 2 ripe pears, peeled and
sliced

Put ice cream in a dish. Arrange pear on top. Pour over the ginger wine. Top with roasted flaked nuts. *Serves 4.*

GINGER ICE-CREAM 1

5 fl. oz (150 ml) hot water
1 tsp. gelatine
10 fl. oz (300 ml) cream
1 tbsp. caster sugar

4 oz (100 g) preserved ginger
2 tbsp. preserved ginger syrup
1 egg white

Dissolve gelatine in hot water, cool. Whip cream and sugar lightly, add the chopped ginger, ginger syrup and cooled gelatine mixture. Stir until all ingredients are well combined. Beat egg white until it forms soft peaks, fold into cream mixture. Pour into freezer tray. Freeze until firm. *Serves 4.*

GINGER ICE CREAM 2

2 pt (1 litre) vanilla ice cream

4 oz (100 g) finely chopped
preserved ginger

Leave the ice cream to soften for a few minutes if very hard. Then turn it out into a chilled bowl and beat in the preserved ginger until well mixed. Cover and freeze again until firm. This dessert freezes well. *Serves 6–8.*

CHOCOLATE GINGER RING

6 eggs
5 oz (150 g) icing sugar
2 tsp. instant coffee

7 oz (200 g) milk or dark cooking
chocolate
6 oz (175 g) peanuts, finely chopped
6 oz (175 g) crystallized ginger

Separate the eggs and whisk the yolks with the icing sugar until they form a frothy mixture. Dissolve the coffee in 1 tsp. hot water and add to the yolks. Melt the chocolate, cool and add to yolks with the peanuts and crystallized ginger. Whip the egg whites until firm and fold evenly into the rest of mixture.

Pour the mixture into a prepared ring mould and bake at 375°F (190°C), Gas Mark 5, in the centre of the oven for 40–45 minutes. Remove carefully from the ring mould when slightly cooled. Serve warm with whipped cream. *Serves 4–6.*

GINGER PEAR FLAN

7 in. (18 cm) pastry case
1 lb (500 g) tinned pears
1 level tbsp. cornflour

3 level tbsp. ginger marmalade
5 fl. oz (150 ml) double cream

Drain pears. Blend cornflour with 2 tbsp. of the juice. Put 6 tbsp. juice into pan with marmalade. Heat gently, thicken with cornflour mixture, bring to boil. Remove from heat and cool. Arrange pears in pastry case and cover with sauce. Decorate with whipped cream or chopped preserved ginger. *Serves 4–6.*

APPLE FLORENTINE

6 oz (175 g) flaky pastry

Filling:
1-1½ lb (450-675 g) crisp dessert
  apples
½ tsp. cinnamon

Spiced ale or cider:
5 fl. oz (150 ml) light ale or
  dry cider
¼ stick cinnamon (about 1-inch,
  2-cm, piece)

icing sugar (for dusting)

1½ oz (37 g) butter
3 oz (75 g) castor sugar
grated rind of ½ lemon

2 oz (50 g) granulated or Demerara
  sugar
¼ tsp. grated nutmeg
pinch of ground ginger
thinly pared rind of ½ lemon

To spice the ale (or cider): pour it into a saucepan and add all the other ingredients; heat slowly until sugar has dissolved, strain and leave to cool. Peel, core and quarter the apples, fry in butter, dusting liberally with sugar. Add cinnamon and grated lemon rind.

Fill 8-inch (20-cm) diameter pie plate with the apples and moisten with a little of the spiced ale (or cider). When cool, cover with flaky pastry rolled out to ½-inch (1-cm) thick and sprinkle with castor sugar. Bake in pre-set oven 400°F (200°C), Gas Mark 6, for 25-30 minutes. Run a sharp knife round the edge to lift crust, then cut into portions. If necessary, add a little more hot spiced cider to moisten apples well. Replace crust, dust with icing sugar and serve warm or hot. *Serves 4-6.*

GINGER BOMBE

2 egg whites
2 oz (50 g) caster sugar
10 fl. oz (300 ml) double cream

1-2 tsp. kirsch or syrup from
  stem ginger
2 oz (50 g) finely chopped stem
  ginger

Oil a bombe mould. Make meringues from the 2 egg whites and caster sugar. When cool break these into small pieces. Whip the cream lightly and flavour it with kirsch or ginger syrup. Fold in the meringue pieces and sprinkle with chopped ginger. Turn into the mould. Cover and place in the freezer for about 3 hours. Turn out the bombe and decorate.

LEMON GINGER PIE

8 oz (225 g) gingernut biscuits
4 oz (100 g) melted butter
10 fl. oz (300 ml) cream

12 oz (350 g) tin condensed milk
5 fl. oz (150 ml) lemon juice

Crush gingernut biscuits and place in sealed jar overnight with slice of bread to soften them. Mix crumbs with butter. Place in a flan dish, press well. Whip cream and condensed milk, then fold in lemon juice, pour into biscuit crust. Decorate with cream and preserved ginger. Chill. *Serves 4.*

GINGER CRUNCH PIE

8 oz (225 g) gingernut biscuits
3 tbsp. melted butter
2 tbsp. ginger syrup
2 tbsp. golden syrup
15 fl. oz (400 ml) water

2 level tbsp. custard powder
2 tbsp. water
1 dessp. gelatine
whipped cream
8 pieces preserved ginger

Grind biscuits and mix with melted butter. Line buttered dish with mixture and allow to set for a few minutes. Put syrups and water in pan and bring to boil. Mix custard powder with water and add to mixture. Stir until transparent. Add gelatine in 1 tbsp. cold water. Cut up ginger and stir into mixture. When cool pour into shell. Decorate with whipped cream and pieces of ginger. *Serves 4.*

LITTLE GINGER CUSTARDS

3 oz (75 g) chopped preserved ginger
10 fl. oz (300 ml) warm milk
3 egg yolks
caster sugar to taste

2 tsp. powdered gelatine
2 tbsp. water
2–3 tbsp. ginger syrup
10 fl. oz (300 ml) double cream

Infuse the chopped preserved ginger in the warm milk. Beat the egg yolks and sugar until liquid and make a thick custard with flavoured milk. Strain. Allow to cool and thicken. Soak the gelatine in the water for 5 minutes and then heat gently to dissolve. Stir the ginger syrup lightly into the cooled custard and dissolved gelatine, stirring again as it cools.

Whip the cream and fold it lightly into the custard before setting. Pour into a prepared mould or individual glasses. *Serves 6.*

GINGER AND RUM MOUSSE

2 tsp. powdered gelatine
1½ tbsp. water
10 fl. oz (300 ml) milk
3 eggs
2 oz (50 g) caster sugar

4 oz (100 g) finely chopped
  preserved ginger
3 tbsp. rum
pinch of salt
pieces of preserved or crystallized
  ginger for decoration

Dissolve the gelatine in the water in the top half of a double boiler or steamer. Bring the milk to a boil. Separate the eggs and beat the yolks with the sugar until pale and thick, add to the milk and mix well. Replace this mixture on a low heat and heat gently, stirring all the time, until it thickens into a custard.

Add the gelatine and finely chopped ginger to the custard. Warm the rum and set it alight; when the flames have died down add to the custard. Leave to cool.

Beat the egg whites with the salt until they stand in peaks, then gently fold into the custard mixture. Put into individual glasses and chill. Decorate the top with the extra ginger pieces. *Serves 6.*

RHUBARB AND GINGER COMPOTE

1-1½ lb (450–675 g) rhubarb
4 oz (100 g) sugar
10 fl. oz (300 ml) water

2 tbsp. preserved ginger syrup
1–2 tbsp. preserved ginger

Trim and cut rhubarb. Put sugar and water into pan and boil rapidly 5 minutes, add ginger syrup. Draw aside, add rhubarb, cover and poach very gently 5–7 minutes. Arrange rhubarb in serving dish, pour over juice and scatter with finely sliced ginger. Chill before serving. *Serves 4.*

RASPBERRIES ROYALE

1 lb (450 g) raspberries
5–10 fl. oz (150–300 ml) ginger wine
a little sugar

Cover raspberries with ginger wine. Sprinkle in a little sugar if desired. Chill for 2 hours. *Serves 4.*

PEARS WITH GINGER SAUCE

15 oz (425 g) tin pears
3 oz (75 g) fine breadcrumbs
2 tbsp. margarine
1 tbsp. butter

1 tbsp. flour
3 tbsp. preserved ginger
3 tbsp. preserved ginger syrup

Drain syrup from pears and reserve. Roll fruit in breadcrumbs and place on baking sheet. Dot with margarine. Bake at 375°F (190°C), Gas Mark 5, until crumbs are browned, about 10 minutes. Meanwhile, make sauce. Melt butter in saucepan. Stir in flour and syrup from pears. Stir until boiling, add chopped ginger and its syrup. Serve pears in hot dish accompanied by sauce in a hot sauceboat. *Serves 4.*

GRILLED PEACHES

4 halved peaches
½ tsp. cinnamon

2 oz (50 g) brown sugar
4 tbsp. ginger wine

Fill stone cavity of peaches with brown sugar and pinch of cinnamon each, pour ginger wine over peaches and set under grill for 10 minutes. Place on hot dish, serve with cream if desired. *Serves 4.*

GINGER FRUIT ORIENTAL

1 lb (450 g) tin sliced peaches
2 tsp. crystallized ginger

10 fl. oz (300 ml) orange juice
2 bananas

Combine peaches, orange juice and ginger, finely chopped. Chill several hours to blend flavours. Peel bananas and run fork down sides to flute. Slice on angle. Add to peach mixture. Heap in serving dishes. *Serves 4–6.*

PEACHES ZANZIBAR

1 lb (450 g) tin peach halves
2 pieces whole ginger
2 3 in. (8 cm) pieces cinnamon
8 whole allspice
4 whole cardamom

6 whole cloves
20 fl. oz (600 ml) vanilla ice-cream
10 fl. oz (300 ml) heavy cream,
  whipped
red and green maraschino cherries

Drain peach juice into a pan, cut ginger into small pieces and add with other spices to juice. Simmer 15 minutes. Arrange peaches in baking dish and pour spiced juice over top. Cover and chill several hours or overnight. Put scoop of ice-cream in coupe or dessert dish. Place peach half over ice-cream and spoon juice over peach. Garnish with whipped cream and pieces of the red and green cherries. *Serves 5–6.*

GOOSEBERRY AND GINGER FOOL

1 lb (450 g) gooseberries, topped
  and tailed
4 tbsp. water
4 oz (100 g) granulated sugar
1 level tsp. ground ginger

10 fl. oz (300 ml) custard,
  freshly made
5 fl. oz (150 ml) double cream
pieces of crystallized ginger
green food colouring

Reserve 8 gooseberries for decoration. Cook remainder slowly with water until very soft and pulpy. Add sugar and stir until dissolved. Simmer gently until most of liquid has evaporated, stirring frequently. Purée in blender if smoother consistency preferred. Combine with custard and ground ginger then leave until cold. Beat half cream until softly stiff and fold into gooseberry mixture. Tint pale green with food colouring, then transfer to 4 sundae glasses. Whip rest of cream until thick. Spoon equal amounts on to each fool then garnish with pieces of fresh ginger and whole gooseberries. Chill well. *Serves 4.*

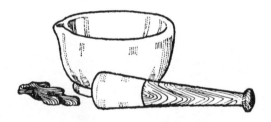

GINGERED FRUIT

15 oz (425 g) tin pineapple pieces
11 oz (300 g) lychees
1 tbsp. chopped glacé cherries

2 tbsp. crystallized ginger
1 oz (25 g) toasted flaked
  almonds

Drain syrup from canned fruits. Lightly combine pineapple, lychees, glacé cherries and ginger in serving bowl. Chill well. Sprinkle almonds on top and serve immediately. *Serves 6–8.*

MANDARINS AND GINGERNUTS

5 fl. oz (150 ml) double cream
1 tsp. castor sugar

8 oz (225 g) gingernut biscuits
11 oz (300 g) tin mandarin
oranges (drained)

Lightly whip cream. Add sugar. Spread layer of broken gingernuts on base of small casserole. Cover this with a layer of mandarin oranges and cover this in turn with a thin layer of whipped cream. Repeat layering until all ingredients are used, finishing with cream. Cover casserole with lid or foil and leave in refrigerator overnight. *Serves 4.*

GINGER BANANA TRIFLES

6 trifle sponge cakes
2 large bananas
juice of ½ lemon
2–3 oz (50–75 g) preserved ginger,
chopped

3–4 tbsp. sweet sherry or sweet
white wine or fruit juice
1 tbsp. ginger syrup
5 fl. oz (150 ml) double cream
2 tbsp. top of the milk

Cut trifle sponges into even-sized cubes. Peel and slice bananas and dip in lemon juice. Arrange sponge cubes, bananas and chopped ginger in 4 individual glasses or dishes. Mix together sherry and ginger syrup and spoon over sponge. Combine cream and milk and whip until thick but still floppy. Spoon over sponge, bananas and ginger. Serve fairly quickly. *Serves 4.*

APRICOT GINGER PARFAITS

8 oz (225 g) dried apricots
4 rounded tbsp. sugar
20 fl. oz (600 ml) water
2 tsp. lemon juice

4 oz (100 g) gingernut biscuits
2 oz (50 g) butter
10 fl. oz (300 ml) cream

Place apricots in bowl. Add sugar and water. Allow to soak overnight. Next day cook for about 10 minutes or until apricots are tender. Purée apricots then stir in lemon juice and set aside until cold. Crush biscuits and pour melted butter over. Whip cream and fold half into apricot mixture. Spoon apricot mixture and crushed biscuits into parfait glasses in alternate layers. Decorate with remaining whipped cream. Chill until serving time. *Serves 4.*

GINGER HASH

15 oz (425 g) tin fruit cocktail
6 oz (175 g) marshmallows
10 fl. oz (300 ml) sour cream

2 tbsp. finely chopped ginger
2 tbsp. toasted almonds

Drain fruit cocktail, combine with marshmallows, sour cream and ginger. Chill for 4 hours. Just before serving, sprinkle with almonds. *Serves 4.*

PINEAPPLE GINGER COUPE

2 bananas
2 tbsp. lemon juice
2 tbsp. preserved ginger, finely diced
few pieces melon, diced
few pineapple cubes, halved

5 fl. oz (150 ml) syrup from
  tinned pineapple
2 tbsp. preserved ginger syrup
5 fl. oz (150 ml) whipped cream

Peel and slice bananas, mix with lemon juice. Add ginger, melon and pine-apple cubes, pineapple and ginger syrups. Chill, until flavours are well blended. Place in glasses and serve with whipped cream.

This recipe is excellent for using up part of an opened can of pineapple. The proportions of fruit used can be varied according to what is available, increasing the number of bananas to three if necessary. *Serves 4.*

GINGER MERINGUE PIE

15 fl. oz (450 ml) milk
2 oz (50 g) fresh breadcrumbs,
  brown or white
grated rind of 1 lemon
2 eggs, separated
1½–2 oz (37–50 g) preserved
  ginger, chopped

1 tbsp. preserved ginger syrup
2 tbsp. apricot jam or jelly
  marmalade, warmed
2–3 oz (50–75 g) castor sugar

Heat milk to just below boiling point. Pour over breadcrumbs in a mixing bowl and leave to stand for about 15 minutes. Beat in lemon rind, egg yolks, ginger and syrup. Turn into ovenproof dish and cook at 350°F (180°C), Gas Mark 4, for about 50 minutes until just set. Spread warmed jam over set breadcrumbs. Whisk egg whites until stiff. Whisk in half sugar. Fold in remainder of sugar and spread or pipe meringue over jam. Return to oven for about 15 minutes until meringue turns pale brown. *Serves 4.*

EGG CUSTARD WITH CHOCOLATE GINGER SAUCE

4 eggs
pinch of salt

20 fl. oz (600 ml) milk
1 oz (25 g) sugar

Chocolate ginger sauce:
2 oz (50 g) grated chocolate
½ oz (12 g) sugar
1 tbsp. ginger wine

10 fl. oz (300 ml) milk
2 level dessp. cornflour

Beat eggs sufficiently to mix yolks and whites, add milk and pinch of salt. Strain into greased pie dish and stir in sugar. Bake for 1 hour at 325°F (170°C), Gas Mark 3, placing piedish in baking tin half filled with water.

To make sauce: put chocolate, sugar, wine and most of milk in pan. Heat gently until chocolate has melted. Mix cornflour to smooth paste with re-maining milk, add to chocolate mixture, stir and boil for about 3 minutes. Serve hot. *Serves 4.*

GINGER PANCAKES

2 eggs, separated
10 fl. oz (300 ml) water
pinch of salt

4 oz (100 g) plain flour
15 fl. oz (400 ml) thick cream
3 tbsp. crystallized ginger

Beat egg yolks, add water, salt and flour, beating constantly. Whip cream and fold it in. Whisk whites to stiff froth and fold in carefully. Fry small thin pancakes. Serve with finely chopped crystallized ginger. *Serves 4.*

GINGER SOUFFLÉ

1½ tbsp. butter
3 tbsp. plain flour
15 fl. oz (400 ml) milk
3 egg yolks
2 tbsp. sugar

2 tsp. cornflour
2–3 tbsp. crystallized ginger
juice of ½ lemon
6–8 egg whites

Fry butter and plain flour until heated through and butter is combined with flour. Add milk and cook basic mixture for 3–5 minutes. Leave to cool a little, stir in egg yolks, one at a time. Add sugar and cornflour. Add ginger and lemon juice. Whisk egg whites stiffly and fold carefully into base mixture. Pour the mixture into well buttered 2½-pint (1·5-litre) dish and bake at 350°F (180°C), Gas Mark 4, for about 40 minutes. Serve immediately with ice cold cream. *Serves 4.*

GINGERED PEARS FOR LOVE

6 ripe pears, peeled
4 oz (100 g) preserved ginger

1 pt (500 ml) ginger wine
3 tbsp. ginger syrup or honey

Thinly slice the peeled pears and preserved ginger, put in a shallow pan and cover with ginger wine mixed with the ginger syrup or honey. Bring to a boil and simmer for about 5 minutes or until the pears are cooked. Serve cold, on their own or with whipped cream. *Serves 6.*

CHOCOLATE GINGER

7 oz (200 g) dark or milk cooking
  chocolate

1 tsp. flavourless salad oil
4 oz (100 g) crystallized ginger

Melt the chocolate with the oil in a bowl over a pan of hot water. With a tooth-pick, dip cubes of crystallized ginger individually into the melted chocolate mixture so that they are completely coated. Place them on greaseproof paper until the chocolate has hardened. Serve as an after-dinner confection and store in a cool place in the refrigerator.

BAKED GINGER FLUFF

4 eggs
3 oz (75 g) sugar
2 tsp. ground ginger
½ tsp. bicarbonate of soda
2 tsp. cinnamon

1 tsp. cocoa
½ tsp. cream of tartar
2 oz (50 g) arrowroot
1 dessp. golden syrup

Beat eggs and sugar for 5 minutes, then add sifted dry ingredients gently, and lastly the golden syrup. Bake in 2 9-inch (22-cm) sandwich tins at 350°F (180°C), Gas Mark 4, 15–20 minutes. Fill with sweetened cream. *Serves 4.*

UPSIDE-DOWN PUDDING

6 oz (175 g) Demerara sugar
4 oz (100 g) butter
3 tbsp. green ginger wine

4 bananas
glacé cherries

Sponge mixture: 2 eggs, their weight in butter, sugar and plain flour with 1½ teaspoons baking powder and some milk.

Melt sugar and butter in an oven dish. Stir in ginger wine and arrange the sliced bananas and cherries in an attractive pattern. For sponge, sift flour and baking powder. Cream butter and sugar. Add eggs, well beaten, a little at a time and keep beating. Add flour gradually, then enough milk to make a soft consistency. Pour sponge mixture over fruit and bake for 1–1¼ hours at 350°F (180°C), Gas Mark 4. When ready turn upside down and serve with whipped cream. As a variant you can use a small tin of pineapple instead of bananas. *Serves 4.*

GINGER MERINGUE DAIRY ICE CREAM

4 oz (100 g) finely chopped
  preserved ginger
3 egg yolks
2 oz (50 g) sugar
10 fl. oz (300 ml) warmed milk

5 fl. oz (150 ml) double cream,
  lightly whipped
3 oz (75 g) meringues
preserved ginger or chocolate
  leaves to decorate

Beat together the egg yolks and sugar until pale, stir in the warmed milk and chopped ginger and stir this custard over a gentle heat, taking care not to allow to come to a boil, until the mixture just coats the back of a spoon. Freeze until mushy.

Next beat the custard well and fold in the lightly whipped cream; freeze again until mushy and beat for the second time.

Break the meringues into pieces and fold into the mixture, place in a 1½-pt (900-ml) bowl and freeze until firm (cover the bowl and freeze for at least another 6 hours). Unmould and decorate with preserved ginger slices or chocolate leaves. *Serves 6.*

PRESERVED GINGER PUDDING

4 oz (100 g) plain flour
2 tbsp. sugar
½ tsp. ground ginger
pinch of salt
2 tbsp. butter

2 oz (50 g) preserved ginger
1 tbsp. golden syrup
10 fl. oz (300 ml) milk
½ tsp. bicarbonate of soda

Mix dry ingredients and rub in butter. Chop preserved ginger and add with golden syrup. Add milk in which soda has been dissolved to make fairly thin batter. Steam in greased covered basin for 2 hours. Serve with custard or ice cream. *Serves 4.*

GINGER SOUFFLÉ 2

a little oil
3 tbsp. butter or margarine
3 tbsp. flour
scant ½ pint (300 ml) hot milk
2 oz (50 g) sugar
4 oz (100 g) finely chopped
crystallized ginger

1 tbsp. ginger-flavoured brandy
(optional)
4 egg yolks, well beaten
5 egg whites, stiffly beaten but
not dry

Oil and then dust with sugar a 4-pt (2-litre) soufflé dish. Melt the butter or margarine in a saucepan, blend in the flour and cook for 2 minutes. Remove from heat. Gradually add the hot milk, stirring to a smooth mixture. Cook and stir over medium heat until the sauce boils and thickens. Remove from the heat and stir in the sugar, ginger, and ginger-flavoured brandy if desired. Let cool for 10–15 minutes.

Add the beaten egg yolks slowly, stirring briskly. Fold in the beaten egg whites gently but thoroughly. Pour into the prepared soufflé dish and bake in an oven preheated to 375°F (190°C), Gas Mark 5, for 40–50 minutes. *Serves 6–8.*

GINGERBREAD PUDDING

3–4 oz (75–100 g) suet
¼ tsp. baking powder
6 oz (175 g) breadcrumbs
2 oz (50 g) flour

1–3 tsp. ground ginger
1 egg
4 oz (100 g) golden syrup

Chop suet finely. Put into basin with baking powder, breadcrumbs, flour and ginger. Mix well together. Beat egg and add syrup. Mix these into dry ingredients and stir until thoroughly mixed. Grease pudding basin and fill with mixture. Cover with buttered paper. Tie with cloth and boil or steam for three hours. When pudding is cooked, turn out on to hot dish. Serve with sweet sauce or custard. *Serves 4.*

GINGER FRUIT PUDDING

4 oz (100 g) stoned raisins
2 oz (50 g) candied peel
3 oz (75 g) butter
3 oz (75 g) breadcrumbs
4 oz (100 g) plain flour
1 tsp. ground ginger

2 well-beaten eggs
1 tsp. lemon juice
2 tbsp. milk
½ tsp. bicarbonate of soda
3 oz (75 g) golden syrup

Sauce:
5 fl. oz (150 ml) honey
½ tsp. grated orange rind
¼ tsp. cinnamon

2 tsp. lemon juice
2 tsp. orange juice

Mix together fruit, butter cut in small pieces, breadcrumbs, flour and ginger. Add eggs, lemon juice and golden syrup, warmed in milk to which bicarbonate of soda is also added. Turn into well-greased basin, tie down with greased paper, and steam for 3½ hours.

Mix all ingredients for sauce and heat through. *Serves 4–6.*

GINGER MADEIRA PUDDING

4 oz (100 g) butter
2 eggs
grated lemon rind
4 oz (100 g) finely chopped
   preserved ginger

4 oz (100 g) caster sugar
6 oz (150 g) self-raising flour
1 tbsp. milk

Wine sauce:
10 fl. oz (300 ml) ginger wine
2 level tsps cornflour

a little water

Beat butter and sugar. Add eggs one at a time and beat until mixture is thick. Stir in sifted flour, ginger, lemon rind and milk. Bake in greased pie dish for 50 minutes at 350°F (180°C), Gas Mark 4.

To make ginger wine sauce: heat wine in pan. Mix cornflour with water, add to wine and stir until it thickens. Serve hot with pudding. *Serves 4.*

GINGER BAKED APPLES

4 medium-size green apples
3 tbsp. finely chopped preserved
   ginger

3 oz (75 g) raisins
2 oz (50 g) brown sugar
2 tbsp. softened butter

Topping
8 oz (225 g) soft cream cheese
scant ½ pint (300 ml) whipped cream

2 tsp. sherry
1 tsp. vanilla essence

Wash and core the apples. Set aside. In a bowl mix together 1 tbsp. of the ginger, the raisins, sugar and butter. Spoon this mixture into the centre of the cored apples. Place on an oven tray and bake in a moderate oven, 350°F (180°C), Gas Mark 4, until cooked. Beat the cream cheese until smooth; add the sherry, vanilla essence and remaining ginger and mix well. Serve as a topping over the warm apples. *Serves 4.*

7
Jams, chutneys and pickles

Whether it is used in a spicy pickle or added to give an extra special flavour to rhubarb jam, ginger is at its most versatile in this section. Hot Indian pickles and chutneys are back in fashion. These are much easier to make than they sound and taste extra good when they are the real home-made thing. When cooked, jams and chutneys should always be bottled in hot, sterilized jars.

ORANGE AND GINGER MARMALADE

5 Seville oranges
5 pt (3 l) water
3 lb (1·35 kg) cooking apples
6½ lb (3 kg) sugar
8 oz (225 g) crystallized ginger
½ oz (12 g) ground ginger

Cut oranges in half and squeeze out juice. Shred peel finely and cut up flesh. Put pips and trimmings into muslin bag in pan with orange peel and flesh, juice and water. Simmer for 1½ hours, and remove bag of pips, squeezing all liquid out. Peel and core apples and cut into slices. Simmer in 4 tbsp. water until pulped. Add apples to oranges and stir in the sugar, until dissolved. Add ginger cut in pieces and ground ginger. Boil rapidly to setting point. Cool slightly, stir well, pour into hot jars and cover.

GINGER MARMALADE

3 lb (1·5 kg) tart apples
1 quart (1·2 litres) water
sugar
1¾ lb (800 g) preserved ginger

Wash and dry apples. Cut into thick slices without peeling or coring. Put all slices into pan with water. Simmer gently till fruit is well pulped, then strain through jelly bag. Allow to drip for several hours. When all juice is in basin, weigh it, and for every pound (450 g) of juice allow 1 lb (450 g) sugar. Turn juice and sugar into preserving pan, and ginger cut into small pieces. Bring to boil. Boil quickly for 8–10 minutes or till preserve sets when tested on a cold plate. Pot and cover while hot.

ELDERBERRY AND GINGER JELLY

4 lb (2 kg) elderberries
¼ pt (150 ml) water
½ oz (12 g) bruised root ginger
juice of 2 lemons

2 oz (50 g) crystallized ginger
3¼ lb (1·45 kg) sugar
1 bottle Certo

Wash and drain fruit, place in pan with water and crush thoroughly. Add bruised root ginger in a muslin bag, and simmer until tender, about 15 minutes. Strain through jelly bag and measure juice into pan. If necessary make up to two pints (1·2 litres) with water. Add sugar, lemon juice and chopped crystallized ginger and heat gently, stirring occasionally until sugar has dissolved. Bring quickly to boil, stir in Certo and boil hard for 1 minute. Remove from heat, skim if necessary, allow to cool slightly. Pot and cover.

GOOSEBERRY, APPLE AND GINGER JELLY

3 lb (1·35 kg) apples
3 lb (1·35 kg) gooseberries
3¼ pt (2 litres) water
1 tsp. ground ginger

6½ lb (2·9 kg) sugar
1 bottle Certo
green colouring (optional)

Remove stems and cut apples into small pieces, but do not peel or core them. Wash gooseberries (no need to top or tail them). Put gooseberries and apples in a large pan with water and ginger. Simmer covered for 20 minutes or until fruit is soft enough to crush. Strain through jelly bag and measure juice into a pan. If necessary make up to 4 pints (2·4 l) with water. Add sugar and heat gently, stirring occasionally until the sugar has dissolved. Stir in Certo, bring to boil and boil rapidly for 1 minute. Remove from heat, skim and stir in the colouring if desired. Pot and cover.

PEAR AND GINGER JAM

3 lb (1·35 kg) ripe Conference pears
3¼ lb (1·45 kg) sugar

4 oz (100 g) crystallized ginger
1 bottle Certo

Peel and core pears. Crush completely (a liquidizer can be used). Put sugar and fruit into large saucepan or preserving pan and mix well. Place on low heat and stir until sugar has dissolved. Add chopped ginger and bring gradually to a full rolling boil. Boil hard for 2 to 3 minutes, stirring at intervals. Remove from heat and stir in Certo. Stir and skim alternately for 3 minutes. Pot and cover.

APPLE AND GINGER JAM

4 lb (2 kg) sugar
3 pt (2 l) water

4 lb (2 kg) apples
2 oz (50 g) root ginger, crushed

Boil sugar and water together until they become syrupy. Peel, core and cut apples into thin slices. Boil ginger (tied in muslin) and apples in syrup until transparent. Remove ginger. Bottle and seal.

MARROW AND GINGER JAM

1 large marrow (approx. 3 lb (1·35 kg))
4 tbsp. water
2 oz (50 g) bruised root ginger
3¼ lb (1·45 kg) sugar

4 oz (100 g) chopped crystallized ginger
2 tbsp: lemon juice
1 bottle Certo

Peel marrow, discarding skin and seeds, and cut up finely. Place marrow in large saucepan with water and simmer, covered, for 20 minutes. Add root ginger (tied in muslin bag), sugar, chopped crystallized ginger and lemon juice; mix well and heat gently, stirring occasionally, until sugar has dissolved. Bring to a full boil for 2 minutes. Remove from heat, take out muslin bag and stir in Certo. Allow to cool to prevent fruit floating. Pot and cover.

MARROW JAM

6 lb (2·7 kg) marrow (peeled and cubed)
grated rind and juice of 4 lemons

3 oz (75 g) root ginger
6 lb (3 kg) sugar
3 pt (1·7 l) water

Put marrow into colander over pan of boiling water. Steam until almost tender. Place in large bowl, and add lemons. Put ginger in a piece of paper, and beat it with a weight. When thoroughly bruised, add it to marrow. (As it has to be removed after cooking, it should be dropped into mixture in a small muslin bag.) Boil sugar and water for seven minutes. Pour over the marrow and leave overnight. Pour into a preserving pan and boil slowly. Cook until marrow is transparent and syrup is thick. Pot and cover.

RHUBARB AND GINGER JAM

3 lb (1·35 kg) rhubarb (weight after trimming)
3 lb (1·35 kg) granulated or preserving sugar
1½ oz (37 g) root ginger
4 oz (100 g) preserved ginger

Cut rhubarb into 2-inch (5-cm) lengths. Fill large bowl with alternate layers of rhubarb and sugar. Cover rhubarb with water. Cover and leave overnight. Transfer rhubarb, sugar and water to large saucepan. Hammer root ginger lightly to bruise it, then tie in a muslin bag. Add to saucepan of rhubarb. Bring slowly to boil, stirring. Boil briskly for 15 minutes. Chop or slice preserved ginger and add. Boil a further 10 to 15 minutes or until rhubarb is clear and setting point is reached. Remove pan from heat, skim off scum and leave to cool. Pot and cover.

SWEET SPICED APPLE PIECES

4 lb (1·8 kg) preserving or
  granulated sugar
2 pt (1·2 l) water
5 fl. oz (150 ml) ginger wine
1 in. (2 cm) cinnamon stick
1 piece mace

small piece ginger root
5–6 cloves
thinly pared rind of 2 lemons
4 lb (2 kg) apples, cored
  and cut into eighths

Boil sugar, water and ginger wine with cinnamon stick, mace, ginger and cloves for 10 minutes. Strain liquid into large clean pan. Add apple pieces and lemon rind; cook until tender, and syrup thick. Add fresh samples of all the spices and pour into sterilized jars, and seal.

RED TOMATO CHUTNEY

6 lb (2·7 kg) large ripe tomatoes
6 onions
6 green peppers
4 oz (100 g) brown sugar
1 tsp. ground mace
1 tsp. ground ginger

4 oz (100 g) salt
1 tsp. ground black pepper
grated rind and juice of 2 lemons
grated rind and juice of 1 orange
15 fl. oz (400 ml) white malt vinegar

Scald and peel tomatoes, cut in half and squeeze to remove most of seeds. Strain these and put liquid into a preserving pan with tomatoes. Thinly slice (or chop) onions. Halve peppers, remove seeds and slice flesh. Add onions and peppers to tomatoes with the rest of the ingredients; stir well and simmer until thick (about 1–1½ hours). When really thick and rich, fill into jars. Tie them down when cold.

APPLE AND TOMATO CHUTNEY

4 lb (1·8 kg) red tomatoes
4 onions, sliced
2 pt (1·2 l) white malt vinegar
1 dessp. peppercorns

1 tbsp. ground ginger
1 oz (25 g) salt
1 lb (450 g) brown sugar
4 lb (1·8 kg) apples

Peel and slice tomatoes, put onions and tomatoes into large bowl, pour
vinegar over and add pepper, ground ginger, salt and sugar. Leave overnight.
Peel, core and slice apples and turn them, with the mixture, into a preserving
pan, stir frequently until boiling and simmer until thick and pulpy, about 1½
hours. Turn into small jars and cover when cold.

SWEET GINGER SAUCE

scant ½ pt (300 ml) water
6 oz (175 g) sugar
juice of 1 lemon

3 tbsp. finely chopped crystallized
  ginger

Put the water, sugar and lemon juice into a saucepan. Cook over a moderate
heat until the syrup spins a thread (230°F (110°C) on a sugar thermometer).
Remove from the heat, stir in the ginger, and bring to boiling point again.
Serve hot or cold over vanilla ice cream or sponge pudding. Made in quantity,
this sauce keeps beautifully. *Makes about 1½ pt (300 ml).*

PIQUANT GINGER SAUCE

Blend finely chopped preserved ginger with chopped fresh garlic, or chopped
fresh garlic and onions, in equal proportions.

The ingredients have to be minced to a fine paste and boiling water added
to bring the paste to the required consistency. Bring to the boil and pack
into jars at minimum 167°F (75°C).

This sauce could be used as a seasoning with any meat or fish dish and is
also excellent as a thickening for gravy.

MANGO GINGER SAUCE

1 lb (450 g) mangoes
6 oz (200 g) finely chopped
  preserved ginger
allspice

salt and pepper
garlic
white vinegar

Mix together the mango and preserved ginger, and add the flavourings to
taste. Bring to a boil and simmer for about 1 hour; you may add boiling
water to obtain a thinner consistency.

You can also add the following to the sauce, during simmering: raisins,
chopped onions, red or green peppers.

Put while still hot into sterilized containers.

PEAR AND GINGER CHUTNEY

3 lb (1·35 kg) pears
1 lb (450 g) onions
1 orange
1 lemon
8 oz (225 g) granulated sugar
4 oz (100 g) seedless raisins

10 fl. oz (300 ml) vinegar
½ tsp. ground cloves
1 tsp. ground ginger
3 dry chilli peppers
1 tsp. salt

Peel, core and chop pears. Chop onions. Grate orange and lemon rinds and squeeze out juice. Bring to the boil with rest of ingredients and simmer for 2 hours. Remove chillis; turn into hot jars and seal.

MARROW CHUTNEY

3 lb (1·35 kg) marrow
salt
12 peppercorns
¼ oz (6 g) bruised ginger
cinnamon and allspice

8 oz (225 g) shallots
8 oz (225 g) green apples
8 oz (225 g) sultanas
1½ pt (900 ml) vinegar
8 oz (225 g) sugar

Cut up marrow and put it into basin. Sprinkle 2 tsp. salt over it and leave for 12 hours. Drain well and rinse. Tie peppercorns, ginger, cinnamon and allspice in muslin bag. Peel shallots and apples. Chop finely. Boil gently all ingredients except sugar. Allow to simmer gently until amost cooked, add sugar and boil until syrupy. Remove spices. Pour mixture into jars and cover.

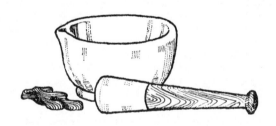

SWEET CHUTNEY

3 lb (1·5 kg) apples
1 lb (500 g) onions
1 lb (500 g) dates, stoned and
    chopped
2 pt (1·2 l) vinegar

2 oz (50 g) ground ginger
pinch cayenne pepper
a few cloves
8 oz (225 g) sugar

Peel, core and chop apples. Peel onions and chop finely. Put all ingredients except sugar together in pan and simmer until tender. Add sugar and continue simmering until a syrupy consistency is obtained. Pour into jars and cover.

GREEN TOMATO CHUTNEY

2 lb (900 g) green tomatoes, peeled
1 lb (450 g), prepared apples
8 oz (225 g) onions
1 oz (25 g) salt
8–12 oz (225–350 g) sugar or treacle

4 oz (100 g) raisins or sultanas
2 pt (1·2 l) vinegar
½ oz (12 g) root ginger
1 tbsp. pickling spice

Remove skins from tomatoes after dipping in boiling water. Peel and core apples. Chop coarsely. Peel onions and slice them. Put spices in muslin bag. Mix all ingredients in pan, except sugar. Bring to boil. Simmer gently, uncovered, until pulp is tender. Add sugar and boil until a syrupy consistency. Remove spices. Pour into a pot and cover at once.

HIGHLAND CHUTNEY

1 large onion
1½ lb (675 g) apples, cored
1 pt (600 ml) malt vinegar
4 oz (100 g) dates
4 oz (100 g) crystallized ginger
8 oz (225 g) raisins

1 lb (450 g) soft brown sugar
¼ level tsp. salt
¼ level tsp. cayenne
¼ level tsp. nutmeg
¼ level tsp. dry mustard

Mince onion and peeled apples coarsely. Boil with vinegar. Reduce heat and simmer for 40 minutes or until apples and onion are pulped. Take pan off heat, mince dates and chop ginger, add to pan with raisins. Stir in brown sugar, salt, cayenne, nutmeg and mustard, cook for 20 to 30 minutes, until chutney thickens.

GRAPEFRUIT AND GINGER MARMALADE

3 large, thin-skinned grapefruit
3 lemons
a piece of root ginger
6 pt (3 litres) water

1 tsp. tartaric acid
5 lb (2¼ kg) warmed sugar
6 oz (175 g) chopped crystallized
ginger

Wash the fruit well and cut in half. Using a grapefruit knife, remove all the flesh and juice and put it into a preserving pan. Tie the pips in a muslin bag with the lemon skins and root ginger; cut the grapefruit skins into short, fairly fine strips and add these to the pan with the water and tartaric acid.

Simmer for 1½ hours or until the peel is very soft and the contents of the pan reduced to about half. Remove the muslin bag and squeeze it well, stir the warmed sugar into the pan until dissolved, put in the crystallized ginger and boil rapidly, stirring slowly, until setting point is reached. Leave to cool until a thin skin forms, stir to distribute the ginger and peel, then pot and seal as usual. *Makes about 8 jars.*

MANGO CHUTNEY

1 pt (600 ml) cider vinegar
12 oz (350 g) brown sugar
2 medium onions, chopped
1 lemon, sliced thin
⅛ tsp. minced garlic
6 oz (175 g) seedless raisins
¼ tsp. cayenne
1½ tsp. salt
6 medium apples, peeled, cored and sliced

1 tbsp. mustard seed
4 oz (100 g) crystallized ginger, thinly sliced
6 tomatoes, peeled and cut into eighths
1 green pepper, chopped
6 whole cloves
¼ tsp. nutmeg
4 large mangoes, peeled and sliced

Combine all ingredients except apples and mangoes in a large saucepan. Cook 1 hour or until liquid is clear and syrupy. Add apples and mangoes; continue cooking until fruit is tender. Fill hot sterilized jars, leaving some head space. Seal. Makes about 5 pints (2¼ litres).

COLONEL GILLESPIE'S KASHMIR CHUTNEY

2 lb (900 g) apples
1 pt (600 ml) vinegar
4 oz (100 g) crystallized ginger
½ oz (12 g) garlic
1 lb (450 g) dates

1 lb (450 g) sultanas
2 lb (900 g) Demerara sugar
2 oz (50 g) salt
½ oz (12 g) cayenne pepper

Leaving skin on apples, core and mince. Boil in half the vinegar, then simmer till just tender. Chop ginger finely, also garlic and dates; then mince all together with sultanas. Add to apples and rest of vinegar, sugar, salt and spices. Simmer until done – about 40 minutes. Fill and seal jars.

APRICOT CHUTNEY

12 oz (350 g) dried apricots
½ pt (300 ml) boiling water
1 lb (450 g) onions, quartered
1 lb (450 g) cooking apples, peeled, cored and sliced
½ pt (300 ml) vinegar

1 level tsp. salt
1 level tsp. mixed spice
½ level tsp. ground ginger
1 level tsp. coriander
12 oz (350 g) granulated or preserving sugar

Pour boiling water over apricots and soak overnight. Drain and mince with onions and apples. Put into saucepan with all remaining ingredients. Stir over low heat until sugar dissolves. Cook, uncovered, until chutney thickens to a jamlike consistency, stirring occasionally. Fill and seal jars.

PICCALILLI

2 cucumbers	1 lb (450 g) onions
1 small- to medium-size marrow	2 cauliflowers
8 oz (225 g) French beans	about 1½ oz (37 g) salt

Pickle:

2 pt (1·2 litres) white malt vinegar	1 oz (25 g) pickling spice
8 oz (225 g) Demerara sugar	1 rounded dessp. ground ginger
1 rounded dessp. turmeric	1 rounded dessp. mustard
1 rounded dessp. flour	

Cut vegetables into small even pieces, put into bowl or dish; sprinkle with salt. Cover and leave for 12 hours; drain. Boil ¾ vinegar with pickling spice for 4–5 minutes, strain. Mix with remaining ingredients and remaining vinegar and return to pan, bring to boil. Add vegetables and mix well. Simmer 10 minutes, draw aside, cool, put into pots and cover.

PICKLE RELISH

24 medium- to large-size cucumbers	1 tbsp. ground turmeric
10 medium-size onions	1 tbsp. celery seed
3 tbsp. salt	1 tbsp. mustard seed
8 oz (225 g) sugar	1 tbsp. ground ginger
3 pt (1·35 l) vinegar	

Wash cucumbers and cover with iced water; let stand 3 hours. Drain; slice cucumbers and onions paper-thin and sprinkle with salt. Allow to stand 3 hours. Drain, reserving 10 fl. oz (300 ml) juice. Combine juice with remaining ingredients; add vegetables. Boil gently until vegetables are clear and transparent, about 40 minutes. Fill hot jars, seal.

GOOSEBERRY CHUTNEY

2½ lb (1.25 kg) gooseberries, preferably not too ripe	2 oz (50 g) fresh ginger
	pinch of ground cloves
1 lemon	1 tsp. curry powder
2 oz (50 g) sugar	1 tsp. tarragon mustard
4 medium onions	2 tbsp. vinegar
1 pt (500 ml) water	1 oz (25 g) honey

Wash the gooseberries well. Grate the rind of the lemon and squeeze its juice. Peel and chop the onions finely.

Bring the water to the boil with the sugar and simmer the gooseberries gently in it until soft. Peel and grate the ginger and add to the gooseberries. Now add the chopped onion, lemon juice and rind, spices, mustard, vinegar and honey. Cook over a low heat in an uncovered saucepan until the chutney thickens, stirring occasionally.

Cool, pack into screw-top jars and store in the refrigerator. This chutney keeps for up to 3 weeks.

RED TOMATO RELISH

6 lb (2·7 kg) ripe tomatoes
2 onions
2 cloves garlic
1 lb (450 g) sugar
10 fl. oz (300 ml) cider vinegar
2 tbsp. plain flour mixed with vinegar

2 tsp. ground ginger
1 tsp. ground mace
1 rounded dessp. chilli powder
1 dessp. dried oregano
2 oz (50 g) salt

Peel and chop tomatoes. Peel and slice onions and garlic. Put all ingredients except flour together into a pan and boil gently for 30 minutes. Blend flour with enough vinegar to make a thin paste, pour into the mixture, and boil for a further 15 minutes, stirring all the time. Cool, then seal the relish in jars.

SPICED CHERRIES

4 lb (1·8 kg) Morello or May Duke
  cherries
1 pt (600 ml) white malt or white
  wine vinegar
2 lb (900 g) granulated sugar

3 roots ginger, bruised
1 stick cinnamon
3–4 cloves
rind of ½ lemon

Stone cherries, put into a big jar. Cover and stand in pan of hot water. Heat gently on top of stove or in oven until cherries are barely tender. Meanwhile simmer together the vinegar, sugar, spices and lemon rind, tied in a muslin bag. Pack cherries into small jars (screw-top honey jars are the best) and add their juice to the liquid in the pan. Remove the spices from this and boil hard to get a thick syrup. Pour this over the cherries and tie or screw down the lids at once.

PICKLED PINEAPPLE

8 oz (225 g) tin pineapple slices
  (unsweetened preferably)
1 tbsp. brown sugar
4 black peppercorns
2 cloves

½ in. (1 cm) stick cinnamon or
  ¼ tsp. powdered cinnamon
2 tbsp. wine vinegar
3 tbsp. grated ginger
pinch of salt

Drain pineapple slices and put them aside. Measure pineapple juice and make up to 5 fl. oz (150 ml) with cold water. Boil juice with rest of ingredients. If using sweetened pineapple, omit sugar. Add pineapple slices after 10 minutes either whole or cut in chunks. Boil for further 10 minutes. Remove pineapple with slotted spoon. Place in shallow bowl. Discard cloves and peppercorns. Continue boiling liquid until syrupy. Pour over pineapple and chill. Serve with cold meats, hams and fish.

CHILLI SAUCE

24 large red-ripe tomatoes	1 tsp. ginger
8 large onions, chopped	1 tbsp. celery seed
6 green peppers, chopped	1 tsp. crushed red pepper
20 fl. oz (600 ml) vinegar	1 tsp. dry mustard
1 tbsp. salt	12 oz (350 g) sugar
1 tsp. cinnamon	1 tsp. cloves

Peel, core and chop tomatoes, combine with remaining ingredients. Boil gently, uncovered, 4 hours or until thickened. Stir frequently to prevent sticking. Fill hot sterilized jars, leaving some head space. Seal. Makes about 6½ pints (3 litres).

CUMBERLAND SAUCE

½ level tsp. prepared mustard	1 level tbsp. cornflour
1 level tbsp. soft brown sugar	2 tbsp. water
¼ level tsp. ground ginger	1 level tsp. each orange and
pinch cayenne pepper	lemon peel
½ level tsp. salt	4 level tbsp. redcurrant jelly
½ pt. (300 ml) red wine (dry)	juice 1 small orange and I small
3 cloves	lemon

Put mustard, sugar, ginger, pepper and salt into pan. Mix to smooth liquid with a little wine. Add rest of wine and cloves. Bring to boil over low heat, stirring continuously. Cover and simmer slowly for 10 minutes. Mix cornflour to smooth cream with water. Add a little wine mixture. Return to saucepan and cook, stirring all the time until sauce comes to boil and thickens. Add all remaining ingredients. Leave over low heat until redcurrant jelly has melted and sauce is hot. Ideal with pork, gammon, offal dishes and roast goose or duck.

CURRY SAUCE

1 medium-size onion, finely sliced	1 in. (2 cm) piece green ginger, scraped
2 tbsp. melted butter	and finely chopped
2 medium-size tomatoes, skinned	pinch cayenne pepper
and chopped	1 tsp. salt
2 cloves garlic, crushed	2 cartons plain yoghourt
2 tsp. curry powder (see p. 13)	5 fl oz. (150 ml) hot water (optional)

Fry onions in butter until pale gold. Add tomatoes, garlic and curry powder. Fry gently for 2–3 minutes. Stir in ginger, cayenne and salt, then mix in yoghourt and simmer for 15 minutes. If thinner sauce is required, add hot water. Adjust seasoning.

8
Drinks

Home-made ginger wine is a great warming drink for a winter's evening. Party punches made from ginger ale have always been favourites. Ginger is also used for health-bringing toddies and is one of the ingredients of England's traditional Wassail.

GINGER WINE

2 lemons
2 Seville oranges
1 gal. (4·8 litres) water
3 lb (1·35 g) sugar
1½ oz (37 g) bruised ginger

2 small tsp. yeast
1 lb (450 g) stoneless raisins
⅛ oz (3⅓ g) isinglass
5 fl. oz (150 ml) brandy

Peel lemons and oranges thinly. Boil peels in water with sugar and ginger for one hour. When liquid has cooled, pour into a cask. Add juice of lemons and oranges, also yeast and raisins. Leave to stand for a week, stirring several times daily. Add isinglass and brandy. Close cask tightly. Leave for six weeks. Strain liquor through muslin and pour into bottles. This wine will improve with keeping. It should be given at least six months for maturing before being used.

DANDELION WINE

dandelion petals to fill a gallon
   (4·8 litre) measure
10 pt (6 l) boiling water
5 lb (2·25 kg) sugar

2 lemons
piece of bruised ginger
a little yeast

Put petals in pan and pour boiling water over them. Stand in cool place, cover and leave for a full two weeks. Stir each day. At the end of that time, strain dandelion liquid through a muslin cloth into large pan. Add sugar to it and stir until dissolved. Rinse lemons, cut into thin slices and put in liquid. Add ginger and bring to boil. Simmer for half an hour. Allow to become almost cold, then spread a little yeast on a slice of toasted bread and put this into the liquid. Cover pan and leave for about four days. Strain the wine. Store in a cask for three or four months. Pour into bottles for use.

ELDERBERRY WINE

2 qt (2·5 l) elderberries
1 gal. (5 l) water
sugar
cloves

a little ginger essence
yeast
brandy

Put berries into water and boil for half an hour. Leave to cool. Press and bruise fruit with wooden spoon. Strain through muslin and measure the extracted juice. Return juice to pan and bring to boil. To each quart of liquid add ¾ lb (350 g) sugar, stirring thoroughly until dissolved. Add cloves and essence and continue to boil quickly for 20 minutes. When cool, pour liquid through strainer into wooden tub. Spread a little yeast on a slice of toast and put it into wine. Wait until the wine settles down and stops 'sizzling', then carefully skim off surface scum. Remove toast and add brandy, apportioning ¼ pt (150 ml) brandy to each gallon of wine. Pour into bottles. Allow at least six months for maturing.

TROPICAL TANTALIZER

4 oz (100 g) chopped preserved
   ginger
7 oz (200 g) sugar
3¾ pt (2 litres) water

4 fl. oz (100 ml) orange juice
5 fl. oz (150 ml) lemon juice
4 fl. oz (100 ml) pineapple juice

Combine the ginger, sugar and water in a large saucepan and simmer for 15 minutes. Cool, add the fruit juices and chill. Serve in glasses decorated with fresh fruit.

REAL GINGER BEER

2 oz (50 g) coarsely grated fresh
   ginger, with the juice
grated peel of 2 limes
6 tbsp. fresh lime juice
8 oz (225 g) light brown sugar

2 pt (1200 ml) boiling water
1 tsp. dry active yeast
2½ fl. oz (75 ml) lukewarm water
2½ fl. oz (75 ml) light rum, or more
   to taste (optional)

In a large pottery bowl, combine the ginger, lime peel, lime juice and sugar, and pour in the boiling water.

In a small bowl, sprinkle the yeast over the lukewarm water and let stand for 2 minutes, then stir the yeast until completely dissolved. Set the bowl in a warm place until it begins to bubble, about 5 minutes.

Add the yeast mixture to the large pottery bowl, cover tightly with a lid or aluminium foil and let stand for 1 week in a warm place. Stir briefly every other day. If using rum, mix in after 5 days. At the end of the week strain the mixture into a glass or ceramic container and cork normally, taking the usual precautions for bottling beer. Allow to stand for 3 days at room temperature, then chill before serving.

RHUBARB CORDIAL

2 lb (900 g) rhubarb
4 oz (100 g) sugar
2 cloves

2 pt (1·2 l) water
¼ oz (6 g) root ginger

Gently simmer chopped rhubarb, sugar, cloves, water and bruised ginger until rhubarb is soft, replacing any water that boils away. Strain well and serve from warmed glass jug decorated with a few mint leaves.

GINGER ALE

1 lb (450 g) white sugar
1 oz (25 g) root ginger, bruised
½ oz (12 g) cream of tartar

1 lemon
1 gal. (5 l) water
2 oz (50 g) yeast

Put sugar, bruised ginger, cream of tartar and lemon rind in bowl. Cover with boiling water. Stir vigorously until sugar is dissolved and allow to cool. Add yeast and lemon juice, cover with thick cloth and leave 24 hours in warm room. Remove the scum, syphon off liquid without disturbing the sediment, and bottle, cork and wire as quickly as possible. The beer is ready to drink in two to three days' time.

TREACLE ALE

1 lb (450 g) golden syrup
8 oz (225 g) black treacle (molasses)
1 gal. (5 l) water

½ oz (12 g) powdered ginger
rind of 1 lemon
2 oz (50 g) yeast

Melt syrup and treacle in boiling water with ginger and lemon rind. When cool, add yeast. Cover bowl or jug with thick cloth and keep in warm room for three days. Syphon off liquid without disturbing the yeast deposit, and bottle. Cork and wire and keep several days before drinking.

OLD ENGLISH CLOUDY GINGER BEER

2 lemons
1 oz (25 g) ginger
3 gal. (14 l) boiling water
1 oz (25 g) cream of tartar

3 lb (1·3 kg) loaf sugar
2 oz (50 g) yeast
1 tbsp. castor sugar

Remove rind from lemons and chop. Extract juice from lemons. Bruise the ginger. Pour boiling water into large crock, and add ginger, cream of tartar, loaf sugar, lemon juice and rind. Mix yeast to cream with castor sugar. When water and other ingredients have cooled to blood heat, add creamed yeast. Stir well, then cover and stand overnight. Carefully remove yeast scum, and bottle. Leave to stand for one or two days before drinking.

GINGER TEA

To each cup, two-thirds filled with warm water, add ½ tsp. ground ginger. Stir well and bring to the boil. Add a tea bag, infuse for a few minutes and add sugar or honey to sweeten.

HONEY MILK SHAKE

1 pt (600 ml) milk
2 tbsp. honey

pinch of cinnamon
pinch of ginger

Combine all the ingredients together thoroughly and serve well chilled, in tall glasses.

WINTER GINGER CORDIAL

8 oz (225 g) figs
½ tsp. allspice
pinch ground ginger
1 saltspoon ground cinnamon
1 saltspoon ground mace
1 saltspoon ground cloves

cold water
3 8½ fl. oz (250 ml) bottles ginger
   ale
1 tsp. cornflour
few drops lemon juice

Stew figs slowly with allspice, ginger, cinnamon, mace, cloves and enough cold water to cover. When figs are tender, remove from stove and press through sieve. Return to clean saucepan. Add ginger ale and heat gradually. Dissolve cornflour in a little water and stir into mixture, stirring constantly until mixture boils. Flavour with a few drops of lemon juice. Serve in small cups with a little chopped candied orange peel floating on top of each.

WASSAIL

2 qt (2·25 l) good ale
½ bottle sherry
½ tsp. each of ground cinnamon,
   ginger and nutmeg

2 strips of lemon rind
8 crab apples, or 3 small
   red apples
soft brown sugar (to taste)

Add sherry, spices and lemon rind to 1¾ qt (2 litres) of the ale and heat, then simmer for 5 minutes. Bake apples until just soft with sugar and baste with remaining ale. Add these to the spiced ale, adding more sugar if necessary. Serve hissing hot in tankards.

MIDSUMMER QUENCHER

10 fl. oz (300 ml) concentrated
  frozen orange juice (undiluted)
5 fl. oz (150 ml) unsweetened
  pineapple juice
5 fl. oz (150 ml) lemon juice

5 fl. oz (150 ml) maraschino juice
10 fl. oz (300 ml) ginger ale
1 level tbsp. honey
1 family brick vanilla ice-cream
2 tbsp. sliced maraschino cherries

Mix fruit juices, maraschino juice, ginger ale and honey well together. Chill thoroughly. Add half ice-cream and stir until blended. Pour into tall glasses. Add tbsp. ice-cream to each then top with cherry slices.

PARTY PUNCH

3 15 oz (425 g) cans pineapple-
  grapefruit juice
1 qt (1·2 l) apple juice
3 cans frozen orange juice
  concentrate or juice of 12 oranges
1 can frozen lemon juice or juice of
  4 lemons
24 whole cloves

4 3 in. (8 cm) pieces cinnamon
½ tsp. ginger
½ tsp. mixed spice
½ tsp. mace
6 cardamom pods
2 oz (50 g) sugar
4 qt (4·8 litres) ginger ale

Combine fruit juices. Tie whole spices in cheesecloth bag and add to juice with other spices and sugar, mix well to dissolve sugar. Let stand several hours. When ready to serve, remove spice bag, stir well. Pour into punch bowl over ice, add ginger ale. Float a spice fruit ring in punch bowl. Makes 2 gallons (9 litres).

SPICE FRUIT RING

small tin pineapple chunks
small tin pineapple rings
small bottle red maraschino
  cherries
small bottle green maraschino
  cherries
1 lemon cut in ¼ in. (⅓ cm) thick slices

few cinnamon sticks
1–2 oranges cut in ¼ in. (⅓ cm) thick
  slices
whole cloves
whole cardamom
1 qt (1·2 l) ginger ale
2 oz (50 g) preserved ginger

Drain pineapple, rinse cherries. Stud outer edges of lemon and orange slices with whole cloves and place whole cardamom in centre. Pour enough ginger ale into ring mould to cover the bottom, freeze. Arrange fruits and whole spices attractively over frozen ginger ale and pour enough ginger ale over fruits and spices to just cover. Freeze. Pour remaining ginger ale into ring mould and freeze until solid. When ready to serve, remove from mould and float in bowl of punch.

GINGER TODDY

1 wineglass ginger wine
juice of half a lemon

1 dessp. honey
boiling water

Pour the wine into a tumbler and add lemon and honey. Top up with boiling water and drink piping hot at bedtime. This is an old-fashioned, but still useful, cure for a cold or a cough.

TEENAGE PARTY PUNCH

20 fl. oz (600 ml) strong Indian or
China tea
1 gal. (5 l) ginger ale

juice of 3 oranges, strained
juice of 2 lemons, strained
1 dessp. Angostura bitters

Mix all ingredients, adding chilled ginger ale just before serving. Float a spice fruit ring (page 78) in the centre of the punch and fresh sprigs of mint and borage, with a few ginger flowers if available.

GINGER PUNCH

3–4 sticks cinnamon
20 cloves
peel of orange
peel of lemon
30 fl. oz (900 ml.) water

3 bottles red wine
1 bottle ginger wine
20 fl. oz (600 ml.) brandy
(optional)

In a muslin bag place cinnamon, cloves and peel. Boil with water for 15 minutes. Strain liquid into large pan and add red wine, ginger wine and brandy (optional). Add sugar to taste, ladle into glasses and serve piping hot.

ORANGE PUNCH

10 fl. oz (300 ml) orange juice
20 fl. oz (600 ml) soda water
sugar syrup to taste

5 fl. oz (150 ml) lemon juice
20 fl. oz (600 ml) ginger ale

Mix ingredients in jug and serve in glasses, each containing ice cubes and thin slices of orange.

QISHR (COFFEE WITH GINGER)

1 pt (600 ml) water
3 tbsp. dark-roasted coffee

3 tbsp. sugar
1 tbsp. ground ginger

Put the water in a coffee pot that can stand on a direct flame. Add the coffee, sugar and ginger and bring to a boil. Remove from the heat, then, when the bubbling stops, return it to the heat and bring to a boil again. Repeat this a third time, then let it rest for 1 minute. Serve the Qishr in very tiny cups.

9
Gingerbread, biscuits and cakes

Ginger snaps, rich ginger cakes, biscuits and gingerbreads are just a few of the many ways of using ginger for a baking day. Ground ginger is used to add spicy flavour to light cakes as well as more substantial cakes for storing, while preserved ginger brings its singular taste to make more exciting fruit cakes.

ANDREW'S GINGERBREAD

12 oz (350 g) plain flour
¼ tsp. salt
1 small dessp. ground ginger
1½-2 eggs

3 oz (75 g) butter or margarine
2 oz (50 g) sugar
3 oz (75 g) golden syrup

Sift flour, salt and ginger. Cream fat, sugar and syrup, and beat in eggs, one at a time. Add sifted flour to make a mixture for rolling. Roll out ⅛-¼ in. (3-6 mm) thick and cut into squares or rounds using a plain 2½-3 in. (5 cm) cutter. Bake on greased baking sheets in a moderate oven (350°F, 180°C, Gas Mark 4) for 20-25 minutes.

GINGER FRUIT CAKE

6 oz (175 g) margarine
6 oz (175 g) caster sugar
2 eggs, beaten
10 oz (275 g) self-raising flour
pinch of salt
2 tsp. ground ginger

4 oz (100 g) sultanas
2 oz (50 g) raisins
4 oz (100 g) chopped preserved
ginger
5-7 tbsp. milk

Cream the margarine and sugar together, add the beaten eggs gradually and beat well. Sift the flour, salt and ground ginger together and fold into the creamed mixture. Add the dried fruit and half the preserved ginger and mix to a soft dropping consistency with the milk.

Turn the mixture into a prepared loaf tin. Place the remaining ginger on the top and sprinkle with caster sugar. Bake in a moderate oven, 350°F (180°C), Gas Mark 4, for about 1½ hours. Leave in the tin until cold.

APPLE GINGER SHORTCAKE

4 oz (100 g) butter
2 oz (50 g) sugar
1 egg

8 oz (200 g) plain flour
½ tsp. baking powder
icing sugar

Filling:
4 green apples
3 tbsp. water
2 whole cloves
2 oz (50 g) sugar

1 in. (2 cm) piece lemon rind
2 oz (50 g) preserved ginger
1 cup sultanas
1 tsp. cinnamon

Cream butter and sugar until light and fluffy, add egg, beat well. Sift flour and baking powder, add to creamed mixture, mix well. Turn on to floured surface, knead until smooth, divide in half. Roll first half into 8 in. (20 cm) round cake tin. Spoon cooled filling over. Roll out second half of pastry; put on top of filling. Prick top of pastry with fork. Bake at 350°F (180°C), Gas Mark 4, 40–45 minutes. Dust top with sifted icing sugar.

Peel, core and thinly slice apples for filling. Put in saucepan with water, cloves, sugar and lemon rind. Bring slowly to boil, cover, reduce heat and simmer gently until apples are cooked. Remove from heat, remove cloves and lemon rind, add finely chopped ginger, sultanas and cinnamon. Return to heat, cook, stirring 3 minutes, cool.

CANADIAN GINGERBREAD

10 oz (275 g) plain flour
2 level tsp. ground ginger
2 level tsp. cinnamon
1 level tsp. bicarbonate of soda
4 oz (100 g) margarine

4 oz (100 g) soft brown sugar
6 oz (175 g) golden syrup
6 oz (175 g) black treacle (molasses)
2 eggs
5 fl. oz (150 ml) boiling water

Sift flour, spices and soda together. Melt margarine, sugar, syrup and treacle gently. Pour into dry ingredients, stir in well-beaten eggs and hot water. Mix well, pour into a prepared 10 in. square (25 × 25 cm) cake tin and bake for 40–45 minutes at 350°F (180°C), Gas Mark 4.

GINGER-NUT MUFFINS

2 eggs, lightly beaten
3 oz (75 g) brown sugar
4 fl. oz (100 ml) vegetable oil
8 fl. oz (250 ml) natural yoghurt
8 oz (225 g) plain flour

1 tsp. baking powder
1 tsp. bicarbonate of soda
4 oz (100 g) crystallized ginger,
    finely chopped
4 oz (100 g) chopped walnuts

Combine the eggs, sugar, oil and yoghurt in a large bowl. In a second bowl mix the flour, baking powder, bicarbonate of soda, crystallized ginger and walnuts. Add the flour mixture to the egg mixture and stir thoroughly. Spoon into 12 prepared bun tins to about three-quarters full. Bake at 400°F (200°C), Gas Mark 6, for 20–25 minutes until golden brown.

GINGERBREAD

4 oz (100 g) butter	pinch of salt
8 oz (225 g) golden syrup	1 tsp. ground ginger
3 oz (75 g) granulated sugar	1 tsp. mixed spice
1 tbsp. orange marmalade	$\frac{1}{2}$ tsp. bicarbonate of soda
5 fl. oz (150 ml) milk	4 oz (100 g) wholemeal flour
4 oz (100 g) self-raising flour	2 small eggs, well beaten

Heat butter, syrup, sugar, marmalade and milk together in pan. Stir gently until sugar dissolves. Allow mixture to cool a little. Meanwhile, sift self-raising flour with salt, spices and soda into mixing bowl, and add wholemeal flour. Mix. Add butter and syrup mixture to beaten eggs. Pour into dry ingredients. Stir with wooden spoon until smooth batter is formed, then pour into 8 in. square (20 × 20 cm) cake tin and bake for 1½ hours, 325°F (170°C), Gas Mark 3. Gingerbread is ready if it springs back into place when pressed with fingertips.

GRASMERE SHORTCAKE

8 oz (225 g) flour	4 oz (100 g) butter
4 oz (100 g) moist brown sugar	$\frac{1}{2}$ tsp. ground ginger

Filling:

8 oz (225 g) icing sugar	small quantity of chopped
2 oz (50 g) butter	preserved bottled ginger
$\frac{1}{2}$ tsp. ground ginger	1 tsp. of the syrup

Place flour, sugar and ginger in bowl and rub in butter until mixture is like breadcrumbs. Have ready a shallow baking tin lined with greased paper and empty mixture into it. Spread evenly with the hand and press very lightly together. Bake at 350°F (180°C), Gas Mark 4, until nicely browned. Turn out and trim edges. Cut in two while still hot. This can be kept in an airtight tin till required.

To make filling: beat butter and sugar to cream, add ground and chopped ginger and syrup. Spread evenly on one piece of cake and press the other piece into position on top.

GINGERBREAD MEN

12 oz (375 g) plain flour
1 tsp. bicarbonate of soda
2 tsp. ground ginger
4 oz (100 g) butter
2 oz (50 g) sugar

4 tbsp. syrup
1 egg, lightly beaten
small pieces of crystallized ginger
  for decoration

Sift the dry ingredients into a bowl, rub in the butter, add the sugar and mix well. Warm the syrup slightly and add with the egg to the other ingredients. Knead until smooth, roll out on a lightly floured surface to ⅛-in. (3 mm) thick and cut out. Lift the men onto a lightly greased baking tray and decorate with crystallized ginger pieces for eyes, nose, mouth and buttons down front of body. Bake in an oven preheated to 375°F (190°C), Gas Mark 5, for 10–15 minutes; then cool on a wire rack.

GINGER ROCKIES

8 oz (225 g) plain flour
pinch of salt
1 tsp. mixed spice
½ tsp. ground ginger
4 oz (100 g) butter or margarine
3 oz (75 g) Demerara sugar

4 oz (100 g) sultanas
2 oz (50 g) crystallized ginger,
  chopped
grated rind of ½ lemon (optional)
1 egg, beaten
milk to mix

Sieve flour, salt, mixed spice and ground ginger into bowl. Add butter and rub in until mixture resembles breadcrumbs. Mix in sugar, sultanas, chopped ginger and lemon rind (if used). Add beaten egg and sufficient milk to mix to stiff dough. Place in rocky heaps on well greased baking sheet and cook at 400°F (200°C), Gas Mark 6, for 20–25 minutes until firm and golden brown. Cool on a wire rack. Makes 10–12. These buns can be drizzled with a little glacé icing made from 2–3 oz. (50–75 g) sieved icing sugar and sufficient lemon juice to give a thick but runny consistency.

GINGER CHIPS

4 oz (100 g) butter or margarine
4 oz (100 g) sugar
1 egg

4 oz (100 g) crystallized ginger
7 oz (200 g) self-raising flour

Melt and brown the butter or margarine, then allow to cool. Add the sugar and beat to a cream. Add the egg and beat again. Add the crystallized ginger and mix well. Stir in the flour. Place spoonfuls on a greased tray and bake in a preheated moderate oven, 350°F (180°C), Gas Mark 4, for about 15 minutes.

GINGER BISCUITS

13 oz (375 g) sugar
10 fl. oz (300 ml) golden syrup
12 oz (350 g) butter
1 tbsp. ginger
1 tsp. cinnamon

1 tsp. ground cloves
10 fl. oz (300 ml) double cream
2 lb (900 g) plain flour
1 tbsp. bicarbonate of soda

Stir sugar and syrup for 10 minutes. Melt butter and add, together with spices. Stir until well mixed. Beat cream for a few minutes and stir in. Mix flour and soda and work in, saving a little flour for rolling out. Knead dough well and keep in cool place overnight. Roll out dough thinly and cut into interesting shapes. Place on buttered baking sheet and bake at 375°F (190°C), Gas Mark 5, until nicely brown.

GINGER SNAPS

8 oz (225 g) butter
9 oz (250 g) caster sugar
9½ oz (270 g) treacle or syrup
2 tsp. ground ginger
¾ tsp. crushed cardamom seeds

1 tbsp. grated bitter orange peel
1 tbsp. minced preserved ginger
2 tsp. bicarbonate of soda
7½ fl. oz (225 ml) double cream
2 lb (900 g) plain flour

Cream the butter, sugar and treacle or syrup until fluffy. Stir in the spices and bicarbonate of soda. Whisk the cream until stiff and work into the mixture, together with most of the flour. Cover with the rest of the flour and chill the dough, preferably until the following day. Work the dough on a table until smooth. Roll out thickly and cut out the biscuits with a cutter.

Place on a greased baking sheet and bake in an oven preheated to 350°F (180°C), Gas Mark 4, for 8-10 minutes. Leave to cool.

BRANDY SNAPS

4 oz (100 g) butter
8 oz (225 g) treacle
5 oz (150 g) plain flour
pinch of salt

1 tsp. ground ginger
6 oz (175 g) sugar
1 tsp. brandy

Melt butter with treacle. Stir in by degrees sieved flour, salt, ginger, sugar and brandy. Mix well. Bake each wafer on a separate greased tin as if several are baked on one tin they are liable to join up. Drop a teaspoonful of mixture on to the centre of the tin, and bake at 375°F (190°C), Gas Mark 5, for about ten minutes. When taken from the oven they will take a moment or so to set. Then, before they commence to harden, ease carefully from the tin with a broad-bladed knife and roll up. If liked, curl round a wooden spoon handle or cornet-shaped mould (for filling with mock cream later). When crisp, store in air-tight tin.

GINGER AND COCONUT BISCUITS

3 oz (75 g) butter or margarine
7 oz (200 g) sugar
1 egg
3 oz (75 g) chopped crystallized
ginger

2 oz (50 g) coconut
8 oz (225 g) self-raising flour

Cream butter and sugar, beat in egg. Stir in ginger and coconut. Add flour and mix well. Form into small balls, set out on greased tray, and depress with the back of a fork. Bake at 350°F (180°C), Gas Mark 4, 15–20 minutes or until lightly browned. Leave on tray until cool. Store in airtight tin.

GINGER CRISPS

3 oz (75 g) butter or margarine
2 oz (50 g) sugar
1 egg yolk
4 oz (100 g) plain flour

1 oz (25 g) crystallized ginger,
finely chopped
2 oz (50 g) cornflakes

Cream together butter or margarine and sugar, add egg yolk then flour and ginger. Knead to soft consistency, adding a little milk if necessary. Form into small balls, roll in cornflakes very slightly crushed, firming on lightly. Place on well-greased oven trays, leaving space for spreading. Bake in moderately hot oven, 425°F (220°C), Gas Mark 7, about 20 minutes or until lightly browned.

GINGER SWISS ROLL

3 standard eggs
5 oz (150 g) caster sugar
3 oz (75 g) self-raising flour
1 level tsp. ground ginger

¼ level tsp. mixed spice
¼ level tsp. ground cinnamon
1 large cooking apple
6 oz (175 g) tin cream

Leave cream in refrigerator overnight. Grease and line Swiss roll tin that measures 13½ in. by 9½ in. (35 cm by 25 cm). Half fill a large pan with water. Bring up to boil then take off heat. Put eggs and ¾ of the sugar in large bowl. Put the bowl over hot water and whisk until mixture holds impression of whisk for 5 seconds. Take bowl off pan and whisk until mixture is cold. Sift flour with spices and fold into egg mixture, a little at a time, using metal spoon. Pour into prepared tin and bake at 425°F (220°C), Gas Mark 7, for 10 minutes or until well risen and firm to the touch. Have ready a sheet of greaseproof paper slightly larger than the cake tin. Sprinkle ½ oz (12 g) sugar on this paper. Trim edges. Roll up with aid of paper. Cool. Meanwhile, peel, core and chop apple. Put in pan with one tbsp. water. Put lid on pan, cook on low heat until soft. Add rest of sugar and cook for 2 minutes. Cool on a plate. Unroll the cake. Spread with cream and apple. Carefully roll up again. Eat the same day.

GINGER SPONGE

4 eggs
3 oz (75 g) castor sugar
2 oz (50 g) arrowroot
4 level tbsp. plain flour
1 tsp. cocoa

2 tsp. ground ginger
$\frac{1}{2}$ level tsp. bicarbonate of soda
1 level tsp. cream of tartar
1 dessp. golden syrup

Separate eggs, beat whites until stiff. Add sugar and beat well until dissolved. Beat in egg yolks. Add sifted dry ingredients. Add warmed golden syrup. Fold all together. Pour into 8 in. (20 cm) sandwich tins. Bake at 350°F (180°C), Gas Mark 4, for 22 minutes. When cold fill with cream.

GINGER CREAM CAKE

3 oz (75 g) butter
2 oz (50 g) castor sugar
2 eggs, separated
6 oz (175 g) self-raising flour
pinch of salt

4 tbsp. milk
1 tbsp. ginger syrup
1 tsp. vanilla essence
1 tbsp. preserved ginger

Frosting:
4 oz (100 g) cream cheese
1 tbsp. milk
1 tbsp. ginger syrup

8 oz (225 g) icing sugar
2 tbsp. preserved ginger

Butter and line a round 7 in. (18 cm) cake tin. Cream butter and sugar together until light and fluffy. Add egg yolks and beat well. Fold in sifted flour and salt alternately with milk, ginger syrup and vanilla essence. Add finely chopped preserved ginger, then fold in stiffly beaten egg whites. Spoon into cake tin. Bake at 350°F (180°C), Gas Mark 4, 50–55 minutes. Turn on to wire tray to cool. Spread frosting thickly over cake and swirl with a fork.

To make frosting: soften cream cheese in warm basin, then cream it with milk and syrup, gradually work in softened icing sugar and chopped ginger.

GINGER COFFEE CAKE

3 oz (75 g) butter
3 oz (75 g) castor sugar
1 large egg
8 oz (225 g) self-raising flour

$\frac{1}{4}$ tsp. salt
1 cup dry ginger ale
3 tbsp. chopped crystallized
  ginger

Topping:
3 tbsp. plain flour
2 tbsp. brown sugar

1 tbsp. butter
$\frac{1}{4}$ tsp. ground ginger

Beat butter and sugar until creamy, add beaten egg, then sifted flour and salt alternately with ginger ale. Add chopped ginger and mix well. Spoon batter into a 9 × 9 in. (22 × 22 cm) slab tin lined and greased with greaseproof paper. Mix topping ingredients to a crumbly consistency and sprinkle over batter. Bake at 350°F (180°C), Gas Mark 4, for 40–45 minutes. Leave in tin for a few minutes before turning out on to paper-covered cooling rack, then turn back so that the crumb topping is uppermost. Serve cut in slices.

GÂTEAU CHINOIS À L'ORANGE

4 oz (100 g) flour
pinch of salt
4 eggs
6 oz (175 g) castor sugar

5–6 sugar lumps
2 oranges
15 fl. oz (450 ml) double cream
2–3 tbsp. sliced glacé ginger

Decoration:
extra double cream
extra glacé ginger, or
   crystallized orange slices

Prepare 2–6 baking sheets in following way: brush with melted lard or oil, dust lightly with flour, then mark an 8 in. (20 cm) circle on each, using plate or pan lid as a guide.

Sift flour with salt. Break eggs into bowl, add sugar and whisk over hot water until mixture is thick and white (if using electric mixer no heat is necessary). Remove from heat and continue whisking until bowl is cold. Fold flour lightly into mixture using metal spoon. Divide mixture into 6 portions and spread each over a circle on prepared sheets (this can be done with fewer sheets in rotation but each time they must be wiped, regreased and floured). Bake at 375°F (190°C), Gas Mark 5, for about 5–8 minutes. Trim each round with sharp knife while still on baking sheet, then lift on to wire rack.

Rub sugar lumps over oranges to remove zest, then pound sugar to a syrup with little orange juice. Whip cream and sweeten with orange syrup. Sandwich 6 rounds of cake with orange cream and sliced ginger. Decorate with extra cream and ginger or crystallized orange slices.

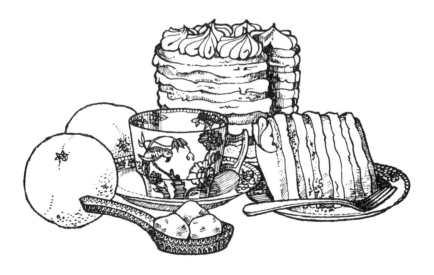

CHOCOLATE GINGER GÂTEAU

3 oz (75 g) butter
3 oz (75 g) castor sugar
2 eggs

Chocolate glacé icing:
4 oz (100 g) icing sugar
2 oz (50 g) butter, unsalted
3 oz (75 g) crystallized ginger

4 oz (100 g) self-raising flour
1 dessp. ground ginger
1 tbsp. chocolate powder

1 tbsp. ginger wine
1 oz (25 g) chocolate powder

Cream butter with sugar, add beaten eggs and flour mixed with chocolate powder and ground ginger alternately. Put mixture into well-greased sandwich tins and bake at 400°F (200°C), Gas Mark 6, for about 20 minutes. When cold, put together with chocolate butter icing (to which has been added 1 oz (25 g) of the crystallized ginger). Make chocolate glacé icing for the top. Decorate round edge with thick slices of crystallized ginger.

DATE AND GINGER LOAF

2 oz (50 g) butter
4 oz (100 g) sugar
2 oz (50 g) chopped dates
2 oz (50 g) chopped preserved
  ginger
10 fl. oz (300 ml) boiling water

$\frac{1}{2}$ tsp. bicarbonate of soda
1 egg, beaten
8 oz (225 g) self-raising flour
pinch of salt
1 tsp. mixed spice

Put butter, sugar, dates, ginger, boiling water and bicarbonate of soda into a bowl, leave for 15 minutes. Add egg. Mix in flour, salt and spice, sifted together. Turn on to greased loaf tin (9 × 3 in. – 22 × 8 cm) and bake at 350°F (180°C), Gas Mark 4, 35–40 minutes. Cut into slices and serve with butter.

PRESERVED GINGER CAKE

5 medium eggs
1¼ lb (500 g) golden syrup, warmed
5 oz (150 g) sugar
6 oz (175 g) butter, softened
1 oz (25 g) ground ginger

1 lb (450 g) plain flour
grated rind of 2 lemons
4 oz (100 g) preserved ginger,
  finely chopped

Beat the eggs well and add the warmed syrup gradually, beating continuously. Add the sugar in the same manner, followed by the softened butter.

Add the ground ginger to the flour, followed by the egg mixture, and beat until bubbles appear, then add the lemon rind and preserved ginger. Bake in a shallow greased tin at 325°F (160°C), Gas Mark 3, for about 2 hours. Cool, cut into squares and keep to mature for a day or so before eating.

GINGER FRUITY PLAIT

8 oz (225 g) self-raising flour
½ tsp. salt
1 oz (25 g) butter
4 tbsp. milk

2 oz (50 g) crystallized ginger
2 oz (50 g) mixed fruit and nuts
1 tbsp. brown sugar
1 dessp. lemon juice

Sieve flour and salt into mixing bowl. Rub butter into flour with fingertips until the mixture resembles fine breadcrumbs. Quickly mix in sufficient milk to make a soft dough. Turn dough on to floured board and knead lightly until smooth. Roll into rectangle 13 × 8 in. (35 × 20 cm). Spread ginger, fruit and nuts down centre of dough, leaving 2 in. (5 cm) margin each side. Sprinkle with brown sugar and lemon juice. Cut each margin into 1 in. strips, slanting downwards from fruit in centre. Brush strips with milk and plait them across fruit mixture. Lift plait on to well greased baking tray. Glaze with milk and bake at 425°F (220°C), Gas Mark 7, 15–20 minutes. When cold, slice and butter.

STICKY GINGER CAKE

4 oz (100 g) butter
4 oz (100 g) soft brown sugar
2 eggs
10 oz (275 g) black treacle
8 oz (225 g) flour

pinch of salt
1 tsp. ground ginger
4 oz (100 g) sultanas (cleaned)
½ tsp. bicarbonate of soda
2 tbsp. warm milk

Cream butter and sugar. Whisk in eggs and treacle. Sift flour with salt and ginger. Using a metal spoon, fold these into mixture, with sultanas. Dissolve bicarbonate of soda in milk and carefully stir into cake mixture. Pour this into prepared cake tin and bake at 325°F (170°C), Gas Mark 3, 1½–2 hours; after 1 hour reduce oven to 300°F (150°C), Gas Mark 2. Cut cake in wedges, spread generously with unsalted butter and top with a good slice of Gouda cheese; reshape into a cake and wrap in foil.

PARSON'S GINGER CAKE

3 oz (75 g) butter
breadcrumbs
2 eggs
6½ oz (187 g) sugar
5 fl. oz (150 ml) sour cream

1½ tsp. ground ginger
2 tsp. cinnamon
1½ tsp. ground cloves
5 oz (150 g) self-raising flour

Butter cake tin and sprinkle with breadcrumbs. Melt butter and allow to cool. Beat eggs and sugar until white and fluffy. Stir in cream and butter. Add spices and flour, stirring until smooth. Pour into cake tin and bake at 375°F (190°C), Gas Mark 5, for about 45 minutes. Allow to cool before turning out of tin.

SOFT GINGER CAKE

3 oz (75 g) rolled oats
5 oz (150 g) self-raising flour
1 tsp. ground cloves
1 tsp. cinnamon

1 tsp. ginger
1 tsp. ground cardamom
10 oz (275 g) sugar
10 fl. oz (300 ml) milk

Butter cake tin and sprinkle with a little flour. Mix oats, flour, spices and sugar. Add milk whilst stirring until smooth. Pour into cake tin. Bake at 375°F (190°C), Gas Mark 5, for about 45 minutes. Cool before turning out.

GINGER DATE CAKE

4 oz (100 g) butter or dripping
5 oz (150 g) golden syrup
2 eggs
12 oz (350 g) plain flour
1 oz (25 g) ground ginger
½ tsp. baking powder

½ tsp. bicarbonate of soda
pinch of salt
milk, if necessary
chopped dates
2 oz (50 g) almonds (optional)

Cream fat and syrup together and beat in eggs. Sieve in the flour, ginger, baking powder, bicarbonate and salt. If necessary add a little milk. Add chopped dates, mix well and pour into greased cake tin. Sprinkle the top, if liked, with blanched and chopped almonds. Bake at 350°F (180°C), Gas Mark 4, for about ¾–1 hour. Cool on wire rack.

HONEY CAKE

8 oz (225 g) honey
4 fl. oz (125 ml) black coffee
1 tbsp. brandy
2 eggs
4 oz (100 g) soft brown sugar
2 tbsp. oil
7 oz (200 g) flour
1 tsp. bicarbonate of soda
½ tsp. ground ginger

½ tsp. grated nutmeg
3 tsp. baking powder
½ tsp. cinnamon
½ tsp. mixed spice
½ oz (12 g) raisins, chopped
½ oz (12 g) dates, chopped
½ oz (12 g) sultanas
1 oz (25 g) almonds (blanched
    and chopped)

Line 2 loaf tins (7½ × 3½ in. – 18 × 8 cm) with greaseproof paper. Mix honey and coffee together in a small pan and bring to boil. Add the brandy; allow to cool. Beat eggs lightly. Stir in the sugar and oil. Sift dry ingredients, and mix with fruit and nuts. Stir flour and honey mixtures alternately into egg mixture until flour is combined. Quickly divide mixture between the two tins. Bake at the centre of the preset oven at 325°F (170°C), Gas Mark 3, for 30 minutes, then reduce the heat to 300°F (150°C), Gas Mark 2, and cook for 40–45 minutes longer. The cake is done when it springs back immediately at the light touch of a finger.

   NOTE: do not open the oven door until at least 1 hour of the cooking time has elapsed. Seal in airtight tin and leave for 2 days before cutting.

GINGER TEA CAKE

4 oz (100 g) butter
2 oz (50 g) sugar
2 eggs
1 tbsp. golden syrup
8 oz (225 g) self-raising flour

1 tsp. cinnamon
1 tsp. ginger
1 tbsp. coconut
5 fl. oz (150 ml) warm water

Cream butter and sugar until light and fluffy, add eggs one at a time, then golden syrup. Sift together flour, cinnamon and ginger, and fold into creamed mixture. Sprinkle on coconut, add water and mix well. Pour mixture into greased 7 in. (18 cm) ring tin and bake at 350°F (180°C), Gas Mark 4, for 45 minutes. Allow to cool on wire rack and serve plain or with butter.

GINGER SOURED CREAM CAKE

6 oz (175 g) soft margarine
6 oz (175 g) soft brown sugar
3 large eggs
6 oz (175 g) self-raising flour

1 tsp. ground ginger
5 oz (150 g) carton soured cream
1 level tbsp. castor sugar

Brush a 7 in. (18 cm) round cake tin with melted fat and line the base with a circle of greaseproof paper cut to fit when greased. Blend margarine, sugar, eggs, sifted flour and ground ginger with wooden spoon, then beat them for a minute until light. Turn mixture into prepared tin and level the surface. Mix soured cream and castor sugar and pour it over the cake. Bake in the middle of the oven at 350°F (180°C), Gas Mark 4, for 1½ hours or until a skewer inserted into the cake comes out clean. If any mixture adheres to the skewer, cook for a little longer. Turn out on to a wire rack to cool.

CHRISTMAS CAKE

8 oz (225 g) butter
8 oz (225 g) brown sugar
4 eggs, beaten
4 tbsp. cold tea or spirits
1 tbsp. black treacle
4 oz (100 g) self-raising flour
¼ tsp. salt
pinch cinnamon
1 tsp. mixed spice
pinch nutmeg

rind of 1 lemon
½ tsp. vanilla essence
6 oz (175 g) plain flour
8 oz (225 g) diced preserved
   or crystallized ginger
2 oz (50 g) peel
8 oz (225 g) sultanas
8 oz (225 g) currants
8 oz (225 g) stoned raisins
2 oz (50 g) cherries

Cream butter and sugar, mix in eggs and tea. Gradually add rest of ingredients with ginger and washed fruit last. Turn into an 8 in. (20 cm) cake tin lined with tin foil and then greased paper. Bake at 300°F (150°C), Gas Mark 2, for 4½ hours or when firm to touch. Cook and wrap in baking foil ready to ice in about 6 to 8 weeks.

SUMMER DAHLIA CHEESECAKE

Base
1½ oz (40 g) margarine
2 tsp. ginger syrup

4 oz (100 g) digestive biscuit crumbs

Filling and topping
4 tbsp. ginger syrup
4 tbsp. water
1 oz (25 g) powdered gelatine
8 fl. oz (250 ml) milk
1 large orange

4 oz (100 g) chopped preserved
  ginger
8 oz (225 g) full-fat soft cheese
2 eggs, separated
1 oz (25 g) caster sugar
angelica strips

Line and grease the base of a 6-in. (15-cm) loose-bottomed cake tin. Melt the margarine and syrup and mix in the crumbs. Press the mixture evenly over the base of the tin; chill while making the filling.

Mix 3 tbsp. of the ginger syrup and the water in a small heat-proof bowl, sprinkle on the gelatine and allow to soften. Stand the bowl in a pan of very hot water and stir until the gelatine dissolves. Stir in 2 tbsp. of the milk and cool to tepid. While cooling, pare off the thin yellow rind of the orange in long strips and cut into neat long slivers. Drop the orange slivers into boiling water for 2 seconds. Drain. Mix the slivers with the remaining tbsp. of ginger syrup and put aside. Remove all white pith from the orange, cut into neat segments without skin or pips, and put aside. Ensure the ginger is finely chopped and put some aside for topping.

Beat the cheese, egg yolks and sugar in a mixing bowl until very soft and creamy. Gradually beat in the tepid gelatine mixture, remaining milk and chopped ginger. Beat hard until completely blended. Whisk the egg whites until they hold soft peaks and fold them in. Turn the mixture gently onto the chilled base and chill again until set. While chilling, drain the orange rind slivers.

To decorate the cheesecake, remove it from the tin. Put the pieces of chopped ginger in the centre. Arrange the orange segments and rind slivers round them like the petals of a flower, with the angelica strips, cut into leaves, between them. *Serves 6.*

GINGER HEALTH CAKE

4 oz (100 g) bran
4 oz (100 g) brown sugar
12 fl. oz (350 ml) milk
4 oz (100 g) walnuts

4 oz (100 g) crystallized ginger
1 tbsp. honey
4 oz (100 g) wholewheat flour
1 tsp. baking powder

Mix together the first 6 ingredients and place in the refrigerator overnight. Then add the wholewheat flour and baking powder. Mix well, form into a cake, place on a greased baking tray and bake for 1½ hours at 350°F (180°C), Gas Mark 4.

Index

94